I0831532

The Poetry of Hanshan (Cold Mountain), Shide, and Fenggan

Library of Chinese Humanities

Acknowledgements

I would like to acknowledge first of all the extraordinary scholarly efforts of the scholar Xiang Chu, whose commentaries on popular Tang poetry are truly exceptional. There would be considerably more doubtful passages and errors in this translation were it not for his groundbreaking work. Second, I owe special thanks to my editor Christopher Nugent, who double-checked my translations, offered suggestions, and showed great patience with my last-minute changes. But as is usual to assert in cases like this, any mistakes in this translation are entirely my own responsibility.

Table of Contents

The Cold Mountain Master Poetry Collection: Introduction

Authorship and reception

The Cold Mountain Master Poetry Collection (*Hanshanzi shi ji* 寒山子詩集) is a corpus of over three hundred poems attributed to a legendary Tang (618–907) era recluse who took the name Hanshan (Cold Mountain) from the isolated hill on which he lived in the Tiantai 天台 Mountains. In pre-modern times, editions of the collection usually included fifty-some poems attributed to Hanshan's monk companion Shide 拾得 ("Foundling") and two poems attributed to another monk, Fenggan 豐干. This translation is a complete rendering of what is generally assumed to be the earliest surviving edition (called by bibliographers the *Song ying ben* 宋影本, "edition printed in the Song"), which was produced before 1170, probably in the 1130s or 1140s; it was reprinted in the *Sibu congkan* series in 1929. There is another line of transmission in which the poems are ordered somewhat differently.

The collection seems to have been widely popular in Chan Buddhist circles in the Song, considering the frequent quotation of lines in Song *yulu* 語錄 ("recorded sayings [of Chan masters]") and the number of legends that that have Hanshan encountering various Chan patriarchs. The Song also saw the beginning of Hanshan verse imitations, authored almost entirely by monastic poets (though the most famous is probably a cycle of twenty poems by the statesman Wang Anshi 王安石 [1021–1086]). The collection spread to Korea, Japan, and Vietnam with the rise of the Chan movement, and attained even greater popularity in those countries. The major Rinzai Zen reformer Hakuin Ekaku 白隱慧鶴 (1686–1768) wrote an extended commentary. Hanshan's modern fame as a participant in "world literature" largely derives from the Beat poet Gary Snyder's encounter with the texts in the 1950s and his selected translations; Snyder's enthusiasm was in turn fictionalized in Jack Kerouac's novel, *The Dharma Bums* (1958).

Date of composition continues to be a mystery. References to the putative authors and to the poems may begin in the ninth century,

DOI 10.1515/9781501501913-004,

though whether these are genuine allusions is open to debate.[1] Two eleventh-century book catalogues mention the collection's existence; one of the listings describes a text likely to be the same as or quite similar to the *Song ying ben* that we have today. Use of internal methods for dating has produced contradictory opinions among scholars, depending partly on the degree to which one assumes that some of the poems are autobiographical (more on this below). Broadly speaking, there tend to be two schools of opinion. Western scholars often cite an article by E. G. Pulleyblank from 1978; in this, he argues that the rhymes in the collection may put two-thirds of the collection in the seventh century or earlier, and that the other third is quite definitely late Tang.[2] Most Chinese scholars follow the bibliographer Yu Jiaxi 余嘉錫 (1884–1955), who argues for the eighth century.[3] It is doubtful that this question will ever be resolved satisfactorily; in any event, the poems' impact on East Asian culture can only be charted from the Song dynasty on.

Much of the debate on the collection's origins revolves around the Preface. It was supposedly composed by an early Tang official by the name of Lüqiu Yin 閭丘胤. The author first describes Hanshan as a lay recluse living at a "Cold Mountain" or a "Cold Cliff." Hanshan occasionally visits the Guoqing 國清 Temple in the Tiantai Mountains, where he has befriended an equally eccentric kitchen monk named Shide. Throughout, Hanshan fits the classic description of the antinomian madman: he annoys the monks with his singing and laughing, until the monks are forced to drive him out. The narrative then turns to Lüqiu himself. Before he embarks on a journey to Tiantai to take up an administrative post, he is cured of a headache by a mysterious monk named Fenggan, also from Guoqing. Fenggan advises him to seek out Hanshan and Shide, and hints that they are the incarnations of bodhisattvas. After Lüqiu arrives at his headquarters, he soon encounters the two men, who merely laugh at him and refuse to talk to him. When he attempts to

1 See, for example, a comprehensive list of possible allusions before the Song era in Chen Yaodong 陳耀東, *Hanshan shi ji banben yanjiu* 寒山詩集版本研究 (Beijing: Shijie zhishi chubanshe), 312–22.

2 E. G. Pulleyblank, "Linguistic Evidence for the Date of Han-Shan," in *Studies in Chinese Poetry and Poetics, Volume 1*, Ronald C. Miao, ed. (San Francisco: Chinese Materials Center, 1978), 163–95.

3 His arguments appear in his monumental *Evidential Analysis of the Catalogue of the Four Treasuries* (*Si ku tiyao bianzheng* 四庫提要辨證), 1937, rev. ed. 1958.

become their patron by supplying them with shelter and basic necessities, they disappear permanently. Hanshan's departure is particularly dramatic: he enters into a mountain cave, which closes up behind him. Lüqiu then commissions one of the Guoqing monks to copy surviving poems by Hanshan and Shide, all of which had been written on the walls of buildings or on trees and cliffs. The narrative obviously contains elements in keeping with monk hagiographies, including gestures toward the fantastic. Yu Jiaxi argues that the text is a forgery: not on the basis of its supernatural elements, but on the basis of its use of anachronistic place names. He dates it to the late ninth century. Most scholars agree with his assessment (regardless of when they think Hanshan lived); but this has not kept nearly everyone from assuming the concrete existence of the three eccentrics.[4] Once one discounts the Preface, the earliest account of Hanshan that may be dated reliably is an anecdote found in the *Comprehensive Records of the Taiping Era* (*Taiping guangji* 太平廣記, ca. 978); it is attributed to a lost work by the Daoist polymath Du Guangting 杜光庭 (850–933), and describes Hanshan as a Transcendent (*xian* 仙).[5] There is also a biography in Zanning's 贊寧 *Biographies of Eminent Monks Composed during the Song Dynasty* (*Song gao seng zhuan* 宋高僧傳; ca. 982), which is essentially a condensed version of the preface.[6]

Faced with such unreliable accounts, many modern scholars have turned to the poems as a source for reconstructing a biography. This is in keeping with the dominant hermeneutics of Chinese poetry reading since at least the Qing dynasty. However, those who attempt such a reconstruction are faced with a bewildering number of events, careers, and life experiences in which the narrative voice seems to have participated—poverty, wealth, military heroism, bureaucratic success and failure, Daoist self-cultivation, contented bucolic reclusion *à la* Tao Qian, community monasticism, and radical Buddhist eremitism—all seem to be within the experience of the supposedly autobiographical

4 One may note that only one poem attributed to Hanshan (HS 40) mentions Shide and Fenggan. FG 1 mentions both Hanshan and Shide. The Shide collection mentions Hanshan in SD 15, 16, and 31, and Fenggan in SD 15.

5 *Taiping guangji*, *juan* 55.

6 Taishō Tripitaka, T. 50, no. 2061, 831b2–832b9. This is a collective biography of Fenggan, Shide, and Hanshan.

speaker (and none of which can be attested by outside historical documents). Many Western readers of Hanshan view him in a similar way, putting the emphasis on his identity as a charismatic dissident. Snyder's championing of the poems resulted in Hanshan becoming a sort of countercultural hero, whose personality was an essential part of his appeal.[7] This essentially autobiographical reading still influences modern Western takes on his poetry. Such a view, though significant as a contribution to modern literature and culture, is largely untenable. There is little evidence that readers before the twentieth century were concerned with discovering traces of a confessional poet in the collection, or that such a reading served as the poems' chief attraction for them.

This also ignores what is probably the most reasonable set of conclusions about the collection—that it was composed by more than one poet over the course of the Tang dynasty (possibly by many poets), that all or most were probably Buddhist monks connected with the Tiantai temple complex, that gradually a myth evolved around the collection that attributed it to a classic antinomian monk precisely at a time when such antinomianism became highly popular in late Tang Chan literature, and that poems were possibly added to the collection later on that deliberately adopted the voice of this monk.

However (as I have argued elsewhere), neither of these perspectives gives us a clue as to how the collection was probably read in pre-modern times.[8] The Preface is quite explicit in identifying Hanshan as an incarnation of the bodhisattva of wisdom, Mañjuśrjī; it also identifies Shide as Mañjuśrī's companion Samantabhadra, and Fenggan as Amitābha. The frequent mention of this identification in later Chan literature (as well as the deification of the three as a popular Chinese cult) suggests that this was more than just a rhetorical gesture. Such an identification leads us in seeing the poems as a form of "skillful means" (*upāya*) meant to aid the believer in attaining his or her spiritual goals.

7 Snyder helped create this persona through the poems he chose to translate: ones in which the poetic voice explicitly names himself or the place that he lives (twenty-one out of the twenty-four). Overall, the collection mentions Hanshan (place or person) in only thirty-nine poems.

8 Paul Rouzer, *On Cold Mountain: A Buddhist Reading of the Hanshan Poems* (Seattle: University of Washington Press, 2015), 51–65.

This view, of course, posits a Buddhist reader, and the collection does seem to have had its greatest impact on the Buddhist community, though Daoists read him with enthusiasm as well. It is not surprising that both groups would find congenial material in the poems. The Tang era saw many syncretic tendencies in the two faiths, and Buddhist and Daoist believers often adopted each other's vocabulary and concepts. Moreover, most Hanshan poems do not explicitly convey a religious message at all, but can be easily redeployed for religious purposes when viewed from a doctrinal perspective (this is characteristic, for example, of many of Hakuin's allegorical readings). However one reads the religious intentions of the poems, it should also be pointed out that a number of "meta-poems" (HS 1, 141, 305, and 313) express the idea that the collection contains a deeper meaning that the wise will uncover through close attention. The poems were probably read as a didactic text, as a source of practical advice, and as a guide for deeper spiritual inspiration and contemplation. As the poet asserts in HS 313:

> If your house has Hanshan's poems,
> That's better than reading the sutras.
> Write them down on a screen,
> And read one now and then.

This didactic aspect is one reason why the collection was not considered "literature" as it was traditionally understood in China. Its closest relations are the Wang Fangzhi 王梵志 collection—a corpus of about four hundred poems found in the Dunhuang manuscripts, and which are primarily popular Buddhist in content; and the poems attributed to Layman Pang 龐 (d. 815), which tend to have more of a Chan flavor. There are elements in Hanshan's style as well that may be found in the *gātha* traditions that were evolving out of the Chan movement (this is especially true of the five-character quatrains: HS 51, 81, 88, 166, 167, 181, 299, 304). None of this poetry, though, could remotely be perceived as mainstream contributions to the history of Chinese verse.

Style and themes

The collection itself is fairly uniform stylistically: it heavily favors the pentasyllabic octet (248 poems out of 313). This may reflect the increasing influence of the regulated verse form in Tang literature, even though the poems largely ignore regulation and elite parallelism. There are also thirteen heptasyllabic octets; sixteen quatrains (both pentasyllabic and heptasyllabic); twenty-nine pentasyllabic poems longer than eight lines; six poems with trisyllabic lines; and one with irregular lines. Though simple parallelism is common, it often manifests through folk-style repetition (see HS 36 and HS 70 for examples). The poems largely eschew the "tripartite form" described by Stephen Owen,[9] often employing their short length artfully to create small narrative and philosophical vignettes, with the last couplet as a sort of "punch line" (in many cases, a proverb):

> That's a mosquito biting into an iron ox—
> No place for him to sink his teeth! (HS 63)
>
> If you can't be as straight as an arrow,
> At least don't be as bent as a hook. (HS 122)
>
> Once you've closed the eyes of the kestrel,
> The sparrows will dance in their pride. (HS 223)

There are many Tang vernacularisms, though not as many as in the Wang Fanzhi collection. There is also a marked movement away from the parataxis that characterizes elite poetry, especially regulated verse. Instead, poems often contain an argument (narrative or philosophical) that stretches over couplet divisions and may have to be intuited in the absence of subordinating conjunctions:

> Your tattered clothes come from your karma;
> Don't curse the body that you have now.
> If you say they result from the site of your graves,
> Then you're really a complete idiot.
> In the end, when you become a ghost,
> Why would you make your children poor?
> This is quite clear and easy to understand—
> Why are you so unperceptive? (HS 252)

9 Stephen Owen, *The Poetry of the Early Tang* (New Haven, Yale University Press, 1977), 9–11.

Many of the poems share the same phrases and images—not enough to indicate formulaic composition, but enough to suggest a circle of poets who repeatedly used the same rhetorical devices. A fair number of poems (particularly satiric ones) begin with a phrase that introduces the topic to be discussed: "I see the people in this world" (*wo jian shijian ren* 我見世間人), or "There's a kind of fool in the world" (*shi you yi deng yu* 世有一等愚) and variants thereof.

Thematically, the poems fall into a number of obvious groups. Probably the most famous (at least to modern readers) are the poems of radical reclusion, which can be affiliated relatively easily to the hagiography found in the preface. These often mention Cold Mountain (the place) as the site of this reclusion, describing it in mysterious or quasi-mystical terms (e.g., HS 38, 154, 177). HS 9 suggests that the mountain is a state of mind:

> How did someone like me get there?
> Because my mind is not the same as yours.
> If your mind were like mine,
> You'd be able to get to the middle of it. (ll. 5–8)

Hakuin makes this clear in his commentary: "There is no place that is not Cold Mountain, so it is not necessary to enter there; you already are there."[10]

However, these reclusion poems only make up about a fifth of the collection. More typical are verses that convey the received wisdom of society (or, contrarily, satirize that wisdom). Some of these themes are common in pre-Tang poetry, particularly the twin themes of *carpe diem* and *ubi sunt*:

> If you have ale, invite others to drink;
> And if you have meat, call others to eat.
> Whether you come to the Yellow Springs early or late,
> When you're young and hale, you must go all out!

10 *Notes on the Lectures on Cold Mountain's Poems at Icchantika Cave* (*Kanzan shi sendai kimon*) (1741), in *Hakuin Oshō Zenshū*, 4:14–15.

Jade belts only flourish for a time,
And gold hairpins will not adorn you for long.
Gaffer Zhang and Goody Zheng—
Once they're gone, we'll hear no more of them. (HS 53)

Such themes often lead to a certain religious interpretation, found either in the poems themselves or in the context of the collection overall—a Buddhist awareness of Impermanence (*wuchang* 無常) or a Daoist desire to cultivate the art of Transcendence. The result of such contemplation often brings us back to Cold Mountain:

Since I've hidden away at Cold Mountain,
I've been eating fruit, nourishing my life.
What do I have to worry about in this existence?
I pass through this world following my karma.
Days and months pass like a departing stream,
Time is just a flash from a flint stone.
You may change along with Heaven and Earth;
But I'll delight in sitting here on my cliff. (HS 171)

A number of poems offer fairly conventional advice of a non-religious nature. One particularly appalling example suggests how to raise your daughters:

We fear having too many daughters;
But once one is born, we must train her carefully.
Force her head down and compel her to be careful,
Beat her on the back to make her shut her mouth.
If she never understands how to use loom and shuttle,
How can she serve with dustpan and broom?
As Granny Zhang said to her donkey's foals,
"You're not as big as your mother!" (HS 175)

But these are relatively rare. The poetic voices of the poems are much more comfortable with righteous anger, jeremiad, and satire. The chief targets are the wealthy, the ignorant, poor scholars, and venal members of the clergy. Some examples:

The new grain has yet to ripen,
While the old grain's already run out.
So I go to borrow a measure or so,
Hesitating outside of their gate.
The husband comes out, tells me to ask the wife;
The wife comes out, sends me to ask the husband.
Being stingy won't save those who lack;
When your wealth is great, you're even more stupid. (HS 126)

I was rather poor in past days,
But this morning I'm most poor and cold!
Nothing I do works out the way it should,
And everything turns to grief and hardship.
When walking through mud I always slip and fall;
When I attend the season festivals I get indigestion.
And now when I've lost my tortoiseshell cat,
The rats are circling the rice jar. (HS 158)

There's a kind of fool in the world,
Muddle-headed, exactly like an ass.
He may understand what you have to say,
But he's porcine in his greed and lust.
He's a deep one—you can't fathom him,
And his "words of truth" will turn to falsehood.
Who can have a word with him
And convince him to not live here? (HS 75)

To see such poems (as recent scholars have) as autobiographical is to deprive the collection of a distinctive poignancy and wit that is largely absent from Chinese literature until the late imperial period.

Another distinctive category consists of explicitly religious poems. There are verses sympathetic to Daoist practice (e.g., HS 22, 48, 79), but a similar number reject Daoist cultivation (e.g., 39, 220, 248). Buddhist content is much more common. Buddhist themes can be divided broadly into two types. In the first, warnings are offered to those who act without compassion or who are unwilling to face the truth of Impermanence:

How limitless the Three Evil Paths;
Murky and dark without a sun.

Eight hundred years of human life
Don't fill out half a nighttime there.
All the fools of this type
To tell the truth, are really pathetic.
I urge you sir, to seek release,
And acknowledge the Prince of the Dharma. (HS 90)

While greed and selfishness are frequently attacked, meat-eating emerges as one of the principal sins—and often rebirth in a Hell realm is held out as the punishment for carnivores.[11] These religious sermons are frequently found in the Wang Fanzhi collection as well; they may represent the closest the Hanshan collection comes to the most popular forms of didactic verse.

The second type of Buddhist poem conveys a discussion of some doctrinal point, or employs a metaphor to illustrate a Buddhist truth. These poems particularly attracted Chan/Zen readers in later centuries, since most of them focus on the concept of the Buddha Nature (*fo xing* 佛性, *Thatāgata-garbha*) or the primacy of the sudden experience of enlightenment as opposed to gradual practice or good works. The Buddha Nature is often described as a jewel (HS 199, 204, 245), sometimes as the moon (HS 51, 200, 287); at other times it is something mysterious within us that we must learn to identify and contact:

I tell all of you who practice the Way:
Vain to labor your spirit in striving.
People have a pure essence within,
Without a name, without a sign.
Call it and it clearly answers,
Yet has no hidden place to dwell.
Be careful to guard it always—
Don't let it have a spot or scratch. (HS 179)

Those enamored of the antinomian madman of the preface may be disappointed to find that there are relatively few poems that dramatize

11 The frequent mention of this sin in the collection is quite striking. See HS 56, 70, 74, 76, 95, 159a, 186, 207, 233, 260, 269; and SD 2, 4, 5, 12, and 39.

this figure, or that use paradox to critique duality (as in the classical Chan/Zen koan tradition). Nonetheless, there are poems that emphasize the "outsider" status of the speaker (HS 25, 221, 275, 289), both in terms of mainstream society and in terms of the monastic community. HS 187 and 288 self-consciously reject elite poetic style, condemning it as merely a tool used by the ambitious to obtain fame and wealth.

There are a few other poems here and there that do not fall into the categories mentioned above. Worth noting are a number of parable-poems, some of which are open to interpretation (e.g., HS 12, 34, 117, 232). Particularly troubling for pre-modern religious readers may have been a number of mildly erotic poems that draw heavily on popular poetry tropes (HS 23, 35, 50, 60–62).

The Shide Collection

The Shide collection does not add anything substantially new to the mix—none of the poems here (except for the ones that mention the putative poet's friendship with Hanshan) would be surprising if they had been attributed to Hanshan originally. In fact, a number of them are identical to Hanshan poems except for unimportant variants. Buddhist satire (of wicked laypeople and of worldly clerics) seems to be more prevalent here than in the Hanshan collection overall.

Text and translation

As I noted above, this is a complete translation of the *Sibu congkan* edition. This includes the Preface, the biographical notes on Fenggan and Shide, and a few editorial comments.[12] In order to replicate the original reading experience of this edition as closely as possible, I have not substituted variant readings in the Chinese text itself. If my translation accepts a variant reading, I have indicated this in the notes. There are a number of cases where variants yield a more aesthetically satisfying reading, but I have avoiding using these for the sake of consistency;

12 The editor also occasionally included pronunciation notes for obscure characters. These I have not translated.

I usually accept variants only if it makes the meaning of an otherwise garbled poem clear.

Understanding of the collection took a giant leap forward with the publication of Xiang Chu's commentary, which surpasses all previous commentaries in terms of detail and erudition.[13] His familiarity with both secular and sacred sources is awe-inspiring, and I find myself usually agreeing with his reading. I have noted specific cases of indebtedness to him in the appropriate places. I also have adapted his numbering system for the poems.

The Hanshan collection was probably meant for a less erudite audience than the verse of a Wang Wei or Du Fu, but this does not always mean that it is always easy to read today. The poems frequently use vernacular expressions, and they also show a fondness for miscellaneous particles and function words whose exact nuance is at times unclear (one may note for example the frequent use of the word *que* 却 as an adverb or as a verbal complement). In such cases, one must be careful not to tend too much to a character-by-character reading. There are also many poems that are intelligible only through the addition of subordinate clauses, adversatives, hypotheticals, and the like; this is true of all Chinese verse, but is particularly true of such a "chatty" collection of poems that are intent on making an argument or on telling a story. I have not hesitated to add words in my translation in order to make the poems clear, and I am sure that some readers will disagree with my interpretations. I have also not hesitated to explain possible allegorical or symbolic readings in the notes if I think such readings would be obvious to most pre-modern readers.

13 Where there are minor variants I typically follow those used by Xiang Chu 項楚 in his *Hanshan shi zhu fu Shide shi zhu* 寒山詩注附拾得詩注 (Beijing: Zhonghua shuju, 2000). These are the versions that appear in the accompanying Chinese text.

The Poetry of Hanshan (Cold Mountain), Shide, and Fenggan

寒山子詩集序

朝議大夫使持節台州諸軍事守刺史上柱國賜緋魚袋閭丘胤撰

詳夫寒山子者。不知何許人也。自古老見之。皆謂貧人風狂之士。隱居天台唐興縣西七十里。號為寒巖。每於茲地。時還國清寺。

寺有拾得。知食堂。尋常收貯餘殘菜滓於竹筒內。寒山若來。即負而去。或長廊徐行。叫喚快活。獨言獨笑。時僧遂捉罵打趁。乃駐立撫掌。呵呵大笑。良久而去。

且狀如貧子。形貌枯悴。一言一氣理合其意。沉而思之。隱況道情。凡所啟言。洞該玄默。乃樺皮為冠。布裘破弊。木屐履地。是故至人遯跡。同類化物。或長廊唱詠。唯言。咄哉咄哉。三界輪迴。或於村墅與牧牛子而歌笑。或逆或順。自樂其性。非哲者安可識之矣。

DOI 10.1515/9781501501913-005,

Preface to the Poetry Collection of the Cold Mountain Master (Hanshanzi)[1]

Composed by Supreme Pillar of State Lüqiu Yin, Recipient of the Crimson Fish Sack, Gentleman for Court Discussion and Acting Prefect Extraordinary of Taizhou in Charge of Military Affairs

When I investigated this Master Hanshan, I could not determine his place of origin. The local elders all held him to be a poor man and an eccentric scholar. He lived as a recluse on Tiantai, seventy *li* west of the county seat of Tangxing, at a place called Cold Cliff. It was from here that he would often visit the Guoqing Temple.

There was a certain Shide there, who managed the temple refectory. Shide would often store leftover scraps of vegetable refuse in a bamboo tube. If Hanshan happened to stop by, he would carry the tube off with him. Sometimes Hanshan would saunter along the long galleries of the temple, shouting with delight and talking and laughing to himself. Then a monk would come out scold him and try to drive him out with a beating. Hanshan would halt and clap his hands and emit a loud laugh, departing only after some time had passed.

He had the look of a pauper, and he was emaciated in appearance. All at once he would make some brief statement expressing his thinking; and when you pondered on it afterwards, it compared favorably with the Dharma in an obscure fashion. Everything that he uttered manifested a sense of quiescent mystery. He wore a hat fashioned of birch bark; a hempen robe, worn and tattered; and a pair of wooden clogs. For this reason, a perfected man will conceal his traces, appearing like any sort of illusory being. Sometimes as he sang as he paced the galleries. He would only say, "Ho! Ho! The wheel of transmigration in the Three Realms!"[2] Sometimes he would sing and laugh with herd-boys in the villages. Whether he acted perversely or conventionally, he did so only to please his own nature. And who could recognize him save the wise?

---

1 The prose narratives in the collection (this Preface, and the notes on Fenggan and Shide) are written in a rather awkward style and occasionally contain obscure phrases. In places my translation is tentative.

2 The Three Realms (the sense realm, the form realm, and the formless realm) constitute the whole of samsara. Beings within them are still subject to rebirth.

胤頃受丹丘薄宦。臨途之日。乃縈頭痛。遂召日者。醫治轉重。乃遇一禪師。名豐干。言從天台山國清寺來。特此相訪。乃命救疾。師乃舒容而笑曰。身居四大。病從幻生。若欲除之。應須淨水。時乃持淨水上師。師乃噀之。須臾祛殄。乃謂胤曰。台州海島嵐毒。到日必須保護。

胤乃問曰。未審彼地當有何賢。堪為師仰。師曰。見之不識。識之不見。若欲見之。不得取相。迺可見之。寒山文殊。遯跡國清。拾得普賢。狀如貧子。又似風狂。或去或來。在國清寺庫院走使。廚中著火。言訖辭去。胤乃進途。

至任台州。不忘其事。到任三日後。親往寺院。躬問禪宿。果合師言。乃令勘唐興縣有寒山拾得已否。時縣申稱。當縣界西七十里內有一巖。巖中古老見有貧士。頻往國清寺止宿。寺庫中有一行者。名曰拾得。

I was once appointed to a low-ranking official position at Danqiu. Days before my departure, I came down with a bad headache. By the day I was to depart, I was taking increasingly large dosages of medicine. I then encountered a master of meditation named Fenggan, who told me that he was from Guoqing Temple at Tiantai, and that he had come especially to visit me. I asked him to treat my condition. He laughed in an easygoing way. "The body is composed of the Four Elements,[1] and illness arises from illusion. If you wish to get rid of your headache, I will require some clean water." I had some clean water brought to him. He spat it out on me, and immediately the pain went away. He then told me: "Taizhou has a coastal climate and miasmal vapors are common. When you arrive there you must look after your health."

I said, "I have not yet discovered whether the place has any eminent men that would be worthy of honoring as my teacher." Fenggan replied, "If you saw such a person, you would not recognize his importance; or if you did so, he would soon vanish. Rather, if you wish to see such a one, do not go by appearances, and he will appear. Hanshan is Mañjuśrī, who has hidden his traces at Guoqing; and Shide is Samantabhadra. Their features are like those of paupers and madmen, and they wander about, carrying out tasks at the Guoqing storehouses and cloisters, and attending to the kitchen fire." After this he bade me farewell, and I too went on my way.

When I reached Taizhou and took up my office, I did not forget what he told me. Three days later, I personally visited the various temples and cloisters and inquired among the meditation centers. Things were as Fenggan had described. I then had inquiries made whether there was a Hanshan and a Shide in Tangxing. The magistrate there notified me that in that very county, seventy *li* to the west, there was a certain cliff; the elders of that area would see a poor scholar there who would often go to Guoqing to spend the night. There was also a monk named Shide residing at the temple storehouse.

1 Earth, water, fire, and wind.

胤乃特往禮拜。到國清寺。乃問寺眾。此寺先有豐干禪師院在何處。并拾得寒山子見在何處。時僧道翹答曰。豐干禪師院在經藏後。即今無人住得。每有一虎。時來此吼。寒山拾得二人，見在廚中。僧引胤至豐干禪師院。乃開房。唯見虎迹。乃問僧寶德道翹。禪師在日。有何行業。僧曰。豐干在日。唯攻舂米供養。夜乃唱歌自樂。

遂至廚中。竈前見二人向火大笑。胤便禮拜。二人連聲喝胤。自相把手。呵呵大笑叫喚。乃云。豐干饒舌饒舌。彌陁不識。禮我何為。僧徒奔集。遞相驚訝。何故尊官禮二貧士。時二人乃把手走出寺。乃令逐之。急走而去。即歸寒巖。

胤乃重問僧曰。此二人肯止此寺否。乃令覓房。喚歸寺安置。胤乃歸郡。遂製淨衣二對。香藥等。持送供養。時二人更不返寺。使乃就巖送上。而見寒山子。乃高聲唱曰。賊賊。退入巖穴。乃云。報汝諸人。各各努力。入穴而去。其穴自合。莫可追之。其拾得迹沈無所。

I went there especially to pay them my respects. When I arrived, I asked the monks where Fenggan had lived, and also where Hanshan and Shide might be. A monk named Daoqiao replied that Fenggan had lived behind the sutra storehouse; however, no one dared lived there now, because there was usually a tiger who would come there and roar. As for Hanshan and Shide, they happened to be in the kitchen. The monk then led me to Fenggan's lodging. He opened the door, and there was nothing to see except for some tiger tracks. I then asked the monks Baode and Daoqiao what task he had had at the temple. The monks told me that he only had milled grain for temple offerings. At night he would sing to please himself.

I then went to the kitchen. There I saw two men laughing before the stove fire. I paid them my respects. They began to taunt me, one after the other. Then, taking each other by the hand, they laughed and shouted: "Fenggan was a gossip! Since you didn't recognize that *he* was Amitābha, why bother to pay us a visit?" All the monks came hurrying in and were astonished, not knowing why a respected official was treating two paupers with such courtesy. The two of them then ran out of the temple, hand in hand. I commanded that they be followed, but they had already rushed off and had returned to Cold Cliff.

I repeatedly asked the monks, "Do you think the two of them would be willing to stay here?" I had some lodgings found for them, and I sent them a message, requesting that they come back and take up residence. I then returned to my headquarters. I had two sets of monastic robes prepared for them, as well as incense and medicine and other things, to be sent to them as a gift, but the two had yet to return to the temple. I sent a messenger to Cold Cliff to deliver it; when he caught sight of Master Hanshan, Hanshan cried out in a loud voice, "Bandits! Bandits!" He then retreated to the mouth of a cave in the cliff and said, "I tell all of you that you should be diligent." He entered the cave and disappeared, and the cave closed up behind him. No one was able to follow him. Shide too disappeared.

乃令僧道翹尋其往日行狀。唯於竹木石壁書詩。并村墅人家廳壁上所書文句三百餘首。及拾得於土地堂壁上書言偈。並纂集成卷。但胤棲心佛理。幸逢道人。乃為讚曰。

菩薩遯迹，
示同貧士。
獨居寒山，
自樂其志。
貌悴形枯，
布裘弊止。
出言成章，
諦實至理。
凡人不測，
謂風狂子。
時來天台，
入國清寺。
徐步長廊，
呵呵撫指。
或走或立，
喃喃獨語。
所食廚中，
殘飯菜滓。

I commanded Daoqiao to search all the places that he had frequented; there were only some poems written on bamboos or on stone cliffs, and verses written on the walls of villagers' dwellings—over three hundred in number. There were also some *gāthas* that Shide had composed on the walls of the shrine to the local earth god. I compiled these into a scroll. I, who keep my mind dwelling on the Buddha's principles, consider myself fortunate to have met these Men of the Way. I have composed a eulogy to them:

A Bodhisattva concealed his traces,
Showing himself as a pauper.
Alone he dwelt on Cold Mountain,
Delighting his own will.
Emaciated in appearance,
Wearing tattered hempen robes.
Every utterance formed a pattern
Whose significance was truly the most perfect understanding.
Ordinary people could not fathom him,
And called him a madman.
Sometimes he would come to Tiantai,
And enter Guoqing Temple.
He would stroll about the galleries,
Laughing, clapping, and pointing,
Sometimes running, sometimes standing,
Muttering to himself.
What he ate in the kitchen:
Table scraps and refuse.

吟偈悲哀，
僧俗咄捶。
都不動搖，
時人自耻。
作用自在，
凡愚難值。
即出一言，
頓祛塵累。
是故國清，
圖寫儀軌。
永劫供養，
長為弟子。
昔居寒山，
時來兹地。
稽首文殊，
寒山之士。
南無普賢，
拾得定是。
聊申讚歎，
願超生死。

He chanted *gāthas* with a shrill tone;
20 Monks and laypeople would scoff and beat him.
But he could never be moved,
So that they became ashamed of their conduct.
In efficacy he was spontaneous,
24 So that ordinary fools could never meet him.
Whenever he uttered a single word,
In an instant he would dispose of samsaric bonds.
For this reason, Guoqing Temple
28 Is planning to set up a customary ritual;
They will make offerings for countless kalpas,
Becoming his disciples forever.
In the past he dwelt on Cold Mountain,
32 But sometimes came to this place.
I do obeisance to Mañjuśrī,
This scholar of Cold Mountain.
And I hail Samantabhadra,
36 Who certainly was Shide.
Let me utter my sighs of praise,
Vowing to transcend life and death.

HS 1

凡讀我詩者，
心中須護淨。
慳貪繼日廉，
諂曲登時正。
驅遣除惡業，
歸依受真性。
今日得佛身，
急急如律令。

HS 2

重巖我卜居，
鳥道絕人迹。
庭際何所有，
白雲抱幽石。
住茲凡幾年，
屢見春冬易。
寄語鐘鼎家，
虛名定無益。

DOI 10.1515/9781501501913-006,

HS 1

All of you who read my poems:
You must guard the purity in your minds.
Daily purify your stinginess and greed;
Forthwith put right your flattering and slyness.
You'll banish all your evil karma,
Take Refuge, receiving your true nature.[1]
Today you'll obtain the Buddha's body—
Be quick, as if this were a command!

HS 2

Mid layered cliffs I chose my home,
A path for birds—cut off from human tracks.
What is there at the edge of my garden?
White clouds embracing the hidden stones.
I have lived here several years together,
And have often seen the seasons change.
I send word to households with their bells and tripods:[2]
No benefit indeed in your empty reputation.

1 *Guiyi* 歸依 ("Take Refuge") is the standard term for accepting the Buddhist teachings.
2 Wealthy families.

HS 3

可笑寒山道，
而無車馬蹤。
聯谿難記曲，
疊嶂不知重。
泣露千般草，
吟風一樣松。
此時迷徑處，
形問影何從。

HS 4

吾家好隱淪，
居處絕囂塵。
踐草成三徑，
瞻雲作四鄰。
助歌聲有鳥，
問法語無人。
今日娑婆樹，
幾年為一春。

HS 3

Delightful is the road to Cold Mountain—
And yet there is no trace of cart or horse.
Impossible to keep track of this network of ravines,
Or to know how many layers of doubled cliffs.
Weeping dew—a thousand kinds of plant;
Moaning in the wind—a solid stretch of pines.
This is when you lose your path,
And your form asks your shadow where to go.

HS 4

My house is well hidden away,
A place to live cut off from clamor and dust.
The trodden plants form three paths here,[1]
While the clouds I see are neighbors in four directions.
There are birds to supply notes to accompany my song,
But no one here to address my Dharma questions.
Today the Shala tree
Makes several years a single spring.[2]

---

1 A poetic cliché for a country recluse's dwelling—there are no regular roads there, but visitors have formed three paths to his door with their passing.

2 Commentators do not agree on the identity of the tree mentioned here, *suopo* 娑婆. This is usually the sinicization of the Sanskrit word *sahā*, a term for our world of suffering (samsara). Xiang Chu suggests that it is an error for *suoluo* 娑羅, or Shala tree (shorea robusta), the tree under which the Buddha's mother gave birth, and also used as a symbol of impermanence. However, the suggestion that it is extremely long-lived suggests a passage in Chapter One of the *Zhuangzi* that describes the *chun* 椿 tree, which takes eight thousand years as a single season of its life. Regardless, the line seems to suggest the readjustment of the recluse's life to a more cosmic frame of time.

HS 5

琴書須自隨，
祿位用何為。
投輦從賢婦，
巾車有孝兒。
風吹曝麥地，
水溢沃魚池。
常念鷦鷯鳥，
安身在一枝。

HS 6

弟兄同五郡，
父子本三州。
欲驗飛鳧集，
須旌白兔遊。
靈瓜夢裏受，
神橘座中收。
鄉國何迢遞，
同魚寄水流。

HS 5

I really should take up calligraphy and zither;
For what use is salary or position?
Heeding wise wife's advice, I abandon my carriage,
And let my filial son drive my cart.
The breeze blows across my threshing floor,
And water fills the pool where I raise fish.
I always am thinking of the wren—
Who is content to rest on a single branch.[1]

HS 6

Like those "brothers," all from five commanderies,
Or the "father and sons" from three prefectures,
I want to prove my piety with a gathering of ducks,
Must mark it with white hares at play.
A magic melon was received in a dream,
A sacred orange was collected from a banquet.
How far away is my homeland!
I drift along the current with the fish.[2]

---

1 A reference to Chapter One of the *Zhuangzi*, in which the modest wren is contrasted with greater and more ambitious creatures.

2 This is the most baffling poem in the Hanshan collection, largely because it consists of a number of allusions strung together. The general import is a paean to filial piety, and I have translated a bit more freely than usual in order to bring the threads together. The narrative voice laments his inability to return home where he can look after his parents. Line 1 refers to a story about five unrelated men from five different places who swore brotherhood and who adopted a beggar woman as their mother. Later, they discovered that she was the mother of the local magistrate, from whom she had been separated when he was still a child. Line 2 similarly refers to three unrelated men who swore to form a family. The third was declared the father; when he made unreasonable demands of them, asking them to build their house in the middle of the river, their filial piety for their "father" resulted in land emerging mysteriously from the water. Lines three and four probably allude to a number of stories relating how birds and rabbits gathered at the mourning huts of filial sons. Line five refers to Jiao Hua 焦華, a filial son who received a magic melon in a dream that subsequently healed his father's illness. Xiang Chu suggests that line six combines two allusions: the story of Wang Lingzhi 王靈之, a filial mourner whose garden produced a magic orange that healed his own illness; and Lu Ji 陸績, who,

HS 7

一為書劍客，
二遇聖明君。
東守文不賞，
4 西征武不勳。
學文兼學武，
學武兼學文。
今日既老矣，
8 餘何不足云。

HS 8

莊子說送終，
天地為棺槨。
吾歸此有時，
4 唯須一番箔。
死將餧青蠅，
吊不勞白鶴。
餓著首陽山，
8 生廉死亦樂。

HS 7

Once I was a student of book and sword,
And twice I encountered sagely lords.
But though I held the east, civil merit went unrewarded,
4 And though I fought in the west, martial deeds were not honored.
I studied civil matters along with the martial ones,
Studied martial matters along with the civil ones.
And today I've already grown old;
8 Of what is left, all is unworthy of mention.

HS 8

Zhuangzi says about bidding farewell to life:
"Make Heaven and Earth your coffin."
When it's time for *me* to "go home,"
4 I'll only need a bamboo mat.
When I'm dead, I'll feed the green flies;
No need to bother the white cranes to mourn me.
If I happen to starve on Shouyang Mountain,
8 If I've lived in virtue, I'll be happy to die.[1]

as a child, took some oranges from a banquet held by the warlord Yuan Shu 袁術 to give to his mother.

1 A reference to the two recluses, Boyi 伯夷 and Shuqi 叔齊, who starved to death on Shouyang Mountain rather than change their allegiances from the Shang dynasty to the Zhou. They became model (if controversial) images of Confucian loyalty.

HS 9

人問寒山道，
寒山路不通。
夏天冰未釋，
日出霧朦朧。
似我何由屆，
與君心不同。
君心若似我，
還得到其中。

HS 10

天生百尺樹，
翦作長條木。
可惜棟梁材，
抛之在幽谷。
年多心尚勁，
日久皮漸秃。
識者取將來，
猶堪柱馬屋。

HS 9

People ask the way to Cold Mountain;
No road passes through to Cold Mountain.
In the summer the ice never melts;
The sun comes out, but the mists preserve their haze.
How did someone like me get there?
Because my mind is not the same as yours.
If your mind were like mine,
You'd be able to get to the middle of it.

HS 10

Heaven gave rise to a hundred-foot tree
That was cut into long boards.
What a shame! Timber for main-beam and rafter
Has been dumped in some remote valley.
Though many years pass, its mind is still strong;
Its bark peels away as the days go by.
Yet one who knows its value may carry it away,
For it still might be used to prop up a stable.

HS 11

驅馬度荒城，
荒城動客情。
高低舊雉堞，
大小古墳塋。
自振孤蓬影，
長凝拱木聲。
所嗟皆俗骨，
仙史更無名。

HS 12

鸚鵡宅西國，
虞羅捕得歸。
美人朝夕弄，
出入在庭幃。
賜以金籠貯，
扃哉損羽衣。
不如鴻與鶴，
颻颺入雲飛。

HS 11

I drove my horse past the ruined city—
A ruined city that moves this wanderer's heart.
High and low, the old crenelated parapets;
Large and small, the ancient tomb mounds.
Bestirred, the shadow of this lonely tumbleweed,[1]
Amid the drawn-out moans of the mighty trees.
Regrettable, all these commonplace bones,
That will never be recorded in the Transcendents' history.[2]

HS 12

A parrot dwelt in the Western lands,
But came here when snared in a huntsman's net.
Now lovely women play with it day and night,
And it flies in and out of the courtyard curtains.
They've presented it with a golden cage;
Imprisoned! It sheds its feathers.
It can't come up to the swans and cranes
Who flap their wings and go soaring into the clouds.

1 The solitary tumbleweed was a standard image for the isolated or exiled poet.

2 That is, the dead have failed to study Daoism, attain immortality, and become Transcendents (*xian*).

HS 13

玉堂挂珠簾，
中有嬋娟子。
其貌勝神仙，
容華若桃李。
東家春霧合，
西舍秋風起。
更過三十年，
還成苷蔗滓。

HS 14

城中蛾眉女，
珠珮珂珊珊。
鸚鵡花前弄，
琵琶月下彈。
長歌三月響，
短舞萬人看。
未必長如此，
芙蓉不耐寒。

HS 13

Beaded curtains hang in a jade hall;
Within, a lovely maiden dwells.
Her features surpass goddess and Transcendent;
Her glories are like those of peach and pear.
In the eastern house the spring mists gather;
In the western lodge the autumn winds rise.
When thirty years go by again,
She'll be turned into pressed sugar cane.[1]

HS 14

A lovely-browed maid of the town;
Her beaded girdle gleams and jangles.
She toys with a parrot before the flowers,
And plays her pipa under the moon.
Her sustained song echoes for three months;
Her brief dance seen by ten thousand.
But it won't be like this forever:
The lotus can't endure the cold.

1 Cane stalks that have had all their juice pressed out, leaving them dry and wrinkled.

HS 15

父母續經多，
田園不羨他。
婦搖機軋軋，
兒弄口㗻㗻。
拍手摧花舞，
搘頤聽鳥歌。
誰當來歎賀，
樵客屢經過。

HS 16

家住綠巖下，
庭蕪更不芟。
新藤垂繚繞，
古石豎巉嵒。
山果獼猴摘，
池魚白鷺啣。
仙書一兩卷，
樹下讀喃喃。

HS 15

I carry on much of the legacy of my parents;[1]
I don't envy others' fields and gardens.
My wife works her loom—chak chak!
My baby tries to speak—gak gak.
I clap my hands, urging the flowers to dance;
I rest chin in hand, and listen to birdsong.
Who comes to admire and congratulate me?
A woodsman stops by now and then.

HS 16

My house resides beneath the green cliffs;
The weeds in my yard have never been mowed.
Fresh vines hang down, wrapping around;
Old stones thrust up, jagged and sharp.
Monkeys pick the mountain fruits;
White herons pluck up the fish from the pond.
A book of the Transcendents—one or two chapters
I mutter to myself under the trees.

1 This line is somewhat open to interpretation. 續經 here may mean "to carry on an occupation." Some would change 續 to 讀 ("to read") and interpret the line as "I am faithful in reading my parents' scriptures." I think this less likely.

HS 17

四時無止息，
年去又年來。
萬物有代謝，
九天無朽摧。
東明又西暗，
花落復花開。
唯有黃泉客，
冥冥去不迴。

HS 18

歲去換愁年，
春來物色鮮。
山花笑淥水，
巖岫舞青煙。
蜂蝶自云樂，
禽魚更可憐。
朋遊情未已，
徹曉不能眠。

HS 17

No stopping the four seasons;
Years depart and years arrive.
The ten thousand things will change and fade;
The nine Heavens neither decay nor crumble.
The east will brighten and the west will darken;
Flowers will fall, then bloom again.
Only the traveler to the Yellow Springs,[1]
Once departed in darkness, will not return.

HS 18

The year departs, traded for a new year of grief,
Though spring now comes and everything looks new.
Mountain flowers laugh at the clear waters;
Cliffs and peaks dance in the blue mist.
Butterflies and bees speak of their own joy;
Birds and fish are even more charming.
But old friendship's feeling never ends,
And I cannot sleep the whole night.

1 Yellow Springs is the traditional term for the underworld.

HS 19

手筆大縱橫，
身材極瓌瑋。
生為有限身，
死作無名鬼。
自古如此多，
君今爭柰何。
可來白雲裏，
教爾紫芝歌。

HS 20

欲得安身處，
寒山可長保。
微風吹幽松，
近聽聲逾好。
下有斑白人，
喃喃讀黃老。
十年歸不得，
忘却來時道。

HS 19

Your calligraphy may be highly fluent,
Your stature utterly impressive.
In life a bounded body,
In death you become a nameless ghost.
It's been often like this since ancient times,
What use for you to struggle now?
Come up here, among the white clouds,
And I'll teach you the Purple Fungus Song.[1]

HS 20

If you want to find a resting place,
Cold Mountain will keep you long.
A gentle breeze blows the hidden pines:
The closer you come, the better it sounds.
Below them sits a white-haired man
Who's mumbling out Daoist texts.
He's not gone home for ten years now,
For he's forgotten how he came.

1 A song supposedly sung by the "Four Whiteheads of Mount Shang" 商山四皓, four recluses who fled civilization when the cruel first emperor of the Qin established his authority. Originally the song suggested that the four recluses could live off of mushrooms they gathered in the mountains; however, later the text became associated with the use of mountain fungi in the concoction of elixirs of immortality.

HS 21

俊傑馬上郎，
揮鞭指柳楊。
謂言無死日，
終不作梯航。
四運花自好，
一朝成萎黃。
醍醐與石蜜，
至死不能嘗。

HS 22

有一餐霞子，
其居諱俗遊。
論時實蕭爽，
在夏亦如秋。
幽澗常瀝瀝，
高松風颼颼。
其中半日坐，
忘却百年愁。

HS 21

Splendid and handsome, that lad on his horse;
He waves his whip and points to the willows.[1]
He claims that he will not die in the end,
And never looks for ways of escaping this world.[2]
Flowers bloom fine throughout the seasons,
But one day they will all wither.
Clarified butter and rock honey—[3]
These things he cannot taste ere he dies.

HS 22

There's a Master who dines on clouds;
His dwelling disdains visits from the vulgar.
Come to mention it, it's really fresh and cool;
Like autumn in the midst of summer.
Secluded creeks flow trickling on,
Winds howl in the lofty pines.
I'll sit half a day in the midst of this,
And forget the grief of a lifetime.

---

1 Willow trees were often planted around pleasure quarters in traditional Chinese cities; here, it suggests that the youth is living a life of pleasure.

2 Literally, "he will never use ladder or boat"—probably images here for vehicles that will convey him beyond the world of suffering.

3 Delicacies mentioned in the sutras to indicate the delights of enlightenment.

HS 23

妾在邯鄲住，
歌聲亦抑揚。
賴我安居處，
此曲舊來長。
既醉莫言歸，
留連日未央。
兒家寢宿處，
繡被滿銀床。

HS 24

快搒三翼舟，
善乘千里馬。
莫能造我家，
謂言最幽野。
巖岫深嶂中，
雲雷竟日下。
自非孔丘公，
無能相救者。

HS 23

Your handmaid lives in Handan city,
And the notes of my song rise and fall.
Tarry in this place of leisure!
This tune has always lasted long.
And when you're drunk, don't speak of going home—
The day lingers—it's still not done.
My house is a place where you can rest;
Where embroidered coverlets cover the silvered beds.

HS 24

Whether you're swift in rowing one of the three winged boats,[1]
Or skilled in riding a thousand-league horse,
You won't be able to reach my home—
That is to say, it's the most remote.
In my cliff-side caves, in the deepest peaks,
Clouds and thunder descend all day.
I am not like Master Confucius;
I have no skill to save you.

---

1 A winged boat was a type of swift battle craft. They were built in three different sizes.

HS 25

智者君抛我，
愚者我抛君。
非愚亦非智，
從此斷相聞。
入夜歌明月，
侵晨舞白雲。
焉能拱口手，
端坐鬢紛紛。

HS 26

有鳥五色彣，
棲桐食竹實。
徐動合禮儀，
和鳴中音律。
昨來何以至，
為吾暫時出。
儻聞絃歌聲，
作舞欣今日。

HS 25

Wise ones, you've cast me off;
Foolish ones, I cast you off.
I'm not foolish, nor am I wise;
So from now on, I'll have no contact with you.
When night comes, I sing of the bright moon;
When dawn arrives, I dance for white clouds.
How can I keep mouth and hands in order,
And sit in meditation, my hair in a tangle?[1]

HS 26

There is a bird with multi-colored plumage,
Who nests in paulownias and eats bamboo seeds.
Its leisured movements are fit for ceremony,
And its harmonious singing matches the pitch pipes.
Why did it come yesterday?
It has showed itself to us for a time.
If it happens to hear the sounds of string and voice,
It will dance, delighting in today.[2]

---

1 The speaker is unwilling to become a monk and undergo rigorous training that will suppress his natural joy. He will not even shave his head.

2 This riddle-like poem describes the *feng* 鳳 (often translated as a phoenix). Chinese lore notes that it roosts only in the paulownia tree, eats only bamboo seeds, and will show itself at the court of a virtuous ruler. One account has it descending and dancing at the court of a virtuous Zhou dynasty ruler.

HS 27

茅棟野人居，
門前車馬疎。
林幽偏聚鳥，
谿闊本藏魚。
山果攜兒摘，
皋田共婦鋤。
家中何所有，
唯有一牀書。

HS 28

登陟寒山道，
寒山路不窮。
谿長石磊磊，
澗闊草濛濛。
苔滑非關雨，
松鳴不假風。
誰能超世累，
共坐白雲中。

HS 27

Eaves of rush, a rustic's dwelling;
Before my gate, carts and horses are few.
The wood is secluded—it harbors birds throughout;
The valley stream is broad—has always kept fish.
Hand in hand with my son I pick mountain fruit;
Together with my wife I hoe the marshy field.
What is there within my house?
Just a bed frame piled with books.

HS 28

I climb up the Cold Mountain road,
The Cold Mountain road that never ends.
Ravines are long and the rocks pile up;
The streambeds are broad, and the grass grows thick.
The moss is slick—but not from the rain;
The pines moan—but they're not relying on wind.
Who is able to transcend the bonds of this world
And sit together with me amid the white clouds?

HS 29

六極常嬰困，
九維徒自論。
有才遺草澤，
無藝閉蓬門。
日上巖猶暗，
煙消谷裏昏。
其中長者子，
箇箇總無裩。

HS 30

白雲高嵯峨，
淥水蕩潭波。
此處聞漁父，
時時鼓棹歌。
聲聲不可聽，
令我愁思多。
誰謂雀無角，
其如穿屋何。

HS 29

Always we encounter the Six Extremities;[1]
Vain to debate about the Nine Worries.[2]
Men of parts are cast to the weedy marsh,
And even those without talent shut their rustic gates.
The sun rises here, yet the cliffs are still dark;
Mist fades way, though the valley is gloomy.
Here the sons of good families[3]
Must each of them go without trousers.[4]

HS 30

White clouds lofty, toppling on high;
Clear water driven into ripples in the pool.
Here is where I hear the fisherman
Who sings now and then as he plies his oars.
Each note I cannot bear to hear,
For it causes me so many gloomy thoughts!
Who says the sparrow has no beak?
Then how could it break into my house?[5]

---

1 "Six extremities": These are described the Hongfan 洪範 chapter of the *Shangshu*: unnatural death, illness, worry, poverty, physical deformity, and weakness.

2 "Nine worries" has not been satisfactorily explained. The surviving fragment of a text by Cai Yong 蔡邕 suggests that it was an enumeration of the sufferings of poverty. Some commentaries take the phrase to mean "the nine networks," and argue that it is another term for *jiuzhou* 九州, i.e., the Nine Provinces of the empire. In that case, the line would refer to the futility of participating in politics and governance.

3 A Buddhist locution frequently found in sutra translations to indicate the virtuous young sons of householders. The poem situates the term within the rhetoric of Confucian talent-selection.

4 A mark of extreme poverty.

5 The last two lines adapt *Shijing* 17, "Dew on the Path" (行露). Here, the poet seems to interpret it as an image expressing emotional intensity. Alternately, the two lines could be the song that the fisherman is singing, expressing his own grief.

HS 31

杳杳寒山道，
落落冷澗濱。
啾啾常有鳥，
寂寂更無人。
磧磧風吹面，
紛紛雪積身。
朝朝不見日，
歲歲不知春。

HS 32

少年何所愁，
愁見鬢毛白。
白更何所愁，
愁見日逼迫。
移向東岱居，
配守北邙宅。
何忍出此言，
此言傷老客。

HS 31

So remote, the road to Cold Mountain;
So lonely, the banks of the chill stream.
So raucous—birds are always here;
So desolate—no people at all.
So rushing—the wind strikes my face;
So profuse—the snow piles up on my body.
Dawn upon dawn, I don't see the sun;
Year upon year, I know nothing of spring.

HS 32

What is it that grieves the youth?
He grieves to see his temple hair turn white.
But what is there to grieve in this white?
He grieves that his days are hastening on,
Until he is moved to a dwelling at Eastern Dai,[1]
Or keeps his house at North Mang.[2]
How can I bear to utter these words?
These words that grieve an old man.

1 Another name for Mt. Tai in Shandong; one of the five sacred mountains, it was believed to be the site of the court of the underworld.

2 The site of burial grounds for the wealthy north of Luoyang. Commonly used as a poetic substitution for "graveyard."

HS 33

聞道愁難遣，
斯言謂不真。
昨朝曾趂却，
今日又纏身。
月盡愁難盡，
年新愁更新。
誰知席帽下，
元是昔愁人。

HS 34

兩龜乘犢車，
驀出路頭戲。
一蠱從傍來，
苦死欲求寄。
不載爽人情，
始載被沈累。
彈指不可論，
行恩却遭刺。

HS 33

I've heard it said that grief can't be dispelled.
And I always thought these words untrue;
But yesterday morn I drove it away,
And today it once again enveloped me.
A month may end, but the grief can't end;
The year renews, and the grief is new too.
Who would have thought that under this broad felt hat
Is a man who has grieved so long?[1]

HS 34

Two turtles ride in a calf-drawn cart,
Driving out to take their pleasure on the road.
A *gu*-beast suddenly appears at their side,[2]
And desperately wants them to give him a ride.
If they don't take him, they are inhumane;
But once they take him, they'll be unjustly blamed.
Snap your fingers—not worth discussing![3]
Practice kindness and you'll be attacked.

1 This type of hat was frequently worn by men who wished to keep their identity secret. It is mentioned a number of times in Tang sources as worn by those who have failed the examinations (thus keeping their faces covered from shame).

2 A *gu* is a mythical creature created by placing poisonous animals together until they devour each other. The last one left alive is a *gu*, particularly poisonous and deadly. It was supposedly used in assassinations.

3 "Snapping the fingers" tends to express strong emotion in Buddhist texts—amazement, admiration, or sorrow. It appears again in HS 226.

HS 35

三月蠶猶小，
女人來采花。
隈牆弄蝴蝶，
臨水擲蝦蟆。
羅袖盛梅子，
金鎞挑筍芽。
鬬論多物色，
此地勝余家。

HS 36

東家一老婆，
富來三五年。
昔日貧於我，
今笑我無錢。
渠笑我在後，
我笑渠在前。
相笑儻不止，
東邊復西邊。

HS 35

In the Third Month, when silkworms are still small,
Women come out to pick the flowers.
Leaning against walls, they play with butterflies;
At the water's edge they toss things at the frogs.
They carry plums in their gauze sleeves,
And dig up bamboo shoots with their golden hairpins.
They compete in collecting the most pretty things;[1]
"This spot is better than home!"

HS 36

The old lady who lives to the east—
She got rich a few years ago.
In former days she was poorer than me;
Now she laughs at me for being broke.
She laughs at me for being behind,
I laugh at her for being in front.
If we don't stop laughing at each other,
The east side—and the west side too.[2]

1 This line refers to a collecting game popular with young women, in which players compete to gather the greatest number of distinctive plants and flowers (usually referred to as "plant competition" (*dou cao* 鬬草).

2 I.e., neither of us is better than the other.

HS 37

富兒多鞅掌，
觸事難祇承。
倉米已赫赤，
不貸人斗升。
轉懷鉤距意，
買絹先揀綾。
若至臨終日，
吊客有蒼蠅。

HS 38

余曾昔覩聰明士，
博達英靈無比倫。
一選嘉名喧宇宙，
五言詩句越諸人。
為官治化超先輩，
直為無能繼後塵。
忽然富貴貪財色，
瓦解冰消不可陳。

HS 37

Wealthy men are really too busy;
In every affair, it's impossible to please them.
The rice in their granary is already rotting,
4 Yet they won't lend anyone a single measure.
More and more they harbor plots and schemes;
They buy raw silk, but first choose fine damask.[1]
But when it comes to the day of their death,
8 They'll have green flies as their mourners.

HS 38

In the past, I have seen all those clever gentlemen;
Erudite and penetrating, talent outstanding, no one to compare with them.
Once they pass the exams, their splendid fame is bruited through the world;
4 Lines from their pentasyllabic poems surpass those of all others.
In office, their governance and moral authority surpass all predecessors,
They assume that only bunglers could follow in their wake.
But if they should achieve wealth and rank, they'll covet riches and sensual delights:
8 The tiles will shatter, the ice will melt: we simply can't describe it.

1 They pretend to be interested in buying the expensive material (in order to impress the merchant) before settling on the cheaper kind.

HS 39

白鶴銜苦桃，
千里作一息。
欲往蓬萊山，
將此充糧食。
未達毛摧落，
離群心慘惻。
却歸舊來巢，
妻子不相識。

HS 40

慣居幽隱處，
乍向國清眾。
時訪豐干道，
仍來看拾公。
獨迴上寒巖，
無人話合同。
尋究無源水，
源窮水不窮。

HS 39

A white crane holds a bitter peach in its beak,
And he takes a rest every thousand *li*.
He wishes to go to Penglai Mountain,[1]
And he has brought this for his provender.
But before he gets there his feathers snap off and fall,
And his heart grieves as he loses his flock.
He flies back to his nest of old,
Where neither wife nor children recognize him.

HS 40

When I get too used to staying in this remote place,
I'll go off at once to the Guoqing assembly.
Sometimes I take the way to visit Fenggan,
Or often come to see Shide.[2]
Then I return alone and climb Cold Cliff;
There's no one whose talk is congenial!
For I'm searching for water that has no source;
Though a source may run out, this water will not.

1 A mythical island in the eastern sea, said to be home to Daoist immortals.

2 This is the only poem in which the putative author mentions his famous companions.

HS 41

生前大愚癡，
不為今日悟。
今日如許貧，
總是前生作。
今日又不修，
來生還如故。
兩岸各無船，
渺渺難濟渡。

HS 42

璨璨盧家女，
舊來名莫愁。
貪乘摘花馬，
樂搒采蓮舟。
膝坐綠熊席，
身披青鳳裘。
哀傷百年內，
不免歸山丘。

HS 41

In your last life you were greatly foolish,
And that is why you are not enlightened today.
And you're rather impoverished today
All because of things you did in your last life.
And if you don't practice in this life either,
Your next life will be just as before.
There are no boats on either bank;
How broad the river—and so hard to cross!

HS 42

How radiant the maid from the house of Lu!
We have always called her "Don't-Grieve."[1]
She's greedy for riding her flower-picking horse,
And loves to ply the oars of her lotus-gathering boat.
Her knees rest on a mat of glossy bear fur;
Her body is cloaked in green phoenix robes.
But alas! Within a hundred years
She can't avoid returning to a grave mound.

1 The girl "Lu Don't-Grieve" is a stock figure for a beautiful maiden in pre-Tang popular ballads.

HS 43

低眼鄒公妻，
邯鄲杜生母。
二人同老少，
一種好面首。
昨日會客場，
惡衣排在後。
只為著破裙，
喫他殘䴺䴽。

HS 44

獨臥重巖下，
蒸雲晝不消。
室中雖暡靉，
心裏絕喧囂。
夢去遊金闕，
魂歸度石橋。
拋除鬧我者，
歷歷樹間瓢。

HS 43

The wife of Master Zou, from Diyan;[1]
The mother of Mr. Du of Handan:
The two of them are about the same age,
And both of them not bad-looking.
Yesterday they went to a party:
The poorly dressed one was shoved to the back.
Just because she wore a shabby skirt
They made her eat the table scraps.

HS 44

I lie alone below the layered cliffs;
The roiling clouds never fade all day.
It's dark and gloomy in my house,
But my mind is cut off from all the noise.
I dream I leave and stroll by golden towers;
My soul returns, crossing a stone bridge.[2]
I've cast aside all the things that annoy me—
Even the rattling of a gourd in the tree where it hangs.[3]

---

1 The phrase *diyan* here has not been satisfactorily explained. Because it is in parallel position with the city name Handan, the poet is likely indicating a place name, but no such place has been identified.

2 Commentators associate this with a natural bridge formation located at Tiantai Mountain. See also HS 218 and HS 266.

3 The ancient recluse Xu You 許由 used to drink water with cupped hands. Someone presented him with a hollow gourd that he could use as a dipper. After he drank from it, he hung it in a nearby tree for safekeeping. At night, the gourd would strike the tree where it hung and make a noise that Xu You found distracting, so he threw it away.

HS 45

夫物有所用，
用之各有宜。
用之若失所，
一缺復一虧。
圓鑿而方柄，
悲哉空爾為。
驊騮將捕鼠，
不及跛猫兒。

HS 46

誰家長不死，
死事舊來均。
始憶八尺漢，
俄成一聚塵。
黃泉無曉日，
青草有時春。
行到傷心處，
松風愁殺人。

HS 45

Now then: all things have their own use;
When you use them, find what's appropriate for each.
If you use them and you fail to place them right,
Then there's a gap, then there's a loss.
Use a round awl with a square handle—
Alas! what you'll do is vain.
Hualiu may be able to catch a rat,[1]
But he'll never come up to a lame cat.

HS 46

Who can avoid death forever?
Death ever makes all things equal.
Now I realize that a six-foot man[2]
In an instant is reduced to a handful of dust.
There is no dawning day at Yellow Springs,
Though spring will come to the green grass.
I travel to a place that wounds my heart—
The wind in the pines grieves me sore.

1 Hualiu is proverbial as the name for a fine horse.

2 The text has "eight feet," but this is likely based on an older calculation of the foot as about 10 English inches.

HS 47

騮馬珊瑚鞭，
驅馳洛陽道。
自矜美少年，
4 不信有衰老。
白髮會應生，
紅顏豈長保。
但看北邙山，
8 箇是蓬萊島。

HS 48

竟日常如醉，
流年不暫停。
埋著蓬蒿下，
4 曉月何冥冥。
骨肉消散盡，
魂魄幾凋零。
遮莫齩鐵口，
8 無因讀老經。

HS 47

A red roan horse, a coral whip—
He gallops about the Luoyang streets,
This conceited, lovely youth,
Who does not believe that things fade and age.
But his white hair will surely grow,
And how can his rosy face last forever?
Just look there at the North Mang Hills—[1]
There's your Penglai Island![2]

HS 48

I feel as if I'm drunk all day.
The flowing years will not stop for a moment.
We'll be buried under the brambles and thorns,
While the moon of dawn fades darkly above.
Bones and flesh will melt away,
And our souls will seem to wither and die.[3]
Then, even if you were cleverest of all,[4]
You never had a chance to read Laozi's classic.[5]

---

1 Burial grounds outside the capital in Eastern Han times; used as a poetic locution for a graveyard. See also HS 32.

2 The island of the immortals.

3 That is, both the *hun* soul and the various *po* souls—in traditional Chinese belief, these various souls disperse upon death.

4 Literally, "have a mouth that can bite iron."

5 You never studied the art of Immortality. Compare to ending of HS 11.

HS 49

一向寒山坐，
淹留三十年。
昨來訪親友，
太半入黃泉。
漸減如殘燭，
長流似逝川。
今朝對孤影，
不覺淚雙懸。

HS 50

相喚採芙蓉，
可憐清江裏。
游戲不覺暮，
屢見狂風起。
浪捧鴛鴦兒，
波搖瀉鵝子。
此時居舟楫，
浩蕩情無已。

HS 49

Sitting on Cold Mountain all along,
Lingering here for thirty years.
Yesterday I visited kin and friends—
Over half have entered the Yellow Springs.
They slowly lessened like a guttering candle,
Flowed off forever like a passing stream.
This morning I faced my lonely shadow,
And my tears ran down unawares.

HS 50

They call to each other while picking lotuses,
How charming in the clear river's current!
Playing about, they don't notice the dusk,
But they can't help but feel the storm wind rise.
Billows surround the mandarin birds,
Waves are rocking the duck and drake.
Just then as they sit within their boat,
Their agitation just won't end.[1]

1 This poem grows out of the erotic trope of young women picking lotus flowers in boats that is common in Chinese poetry. The image at the end suggests that the storm is an external manifestation of their emotional agitation (probably romantic feelings).

HS 51

吾心似秋月，
碧潭清皎潔。
無物堪比倫，
教我如何說。

HS 52

垂柳暗如煙，
飛花飄似霰。
夫居離婦州，
婦住思夫縣。
各在天一涯，
何時得相見。
寄語明月樓，
莫貯雙飛鷰。

HS 53

有酒相招飲，
有肉相呼喫。
黃泉前後人，
少壯須努力。

HS 51

My mind is like the autumn moon
In a jade-green pool—clear, bright and pure.
Nothing can bear comparison to it—
What would you have me say?

HS 52

Drooping willows are dark as mist,
Flying petals gust like sleet.
The husband lives in Parted-from-Wife Prefecture,
4 The wife dwells in Longing-for-Husband County.
Each at one edge of the sky—
When will they get to see each other again?
Send word to her moonlit mansion—
8 Don't shelter a pair of flying swallows![1]

HS 53

If you have ale, invite others to drink;
And if you have meat, call others to eat.
Whether you come to the Yellow Springs early or late,
4 When you're young and hale, you must go all out!

---

1 Pairs of swallows nesting in the beams of a house in springtime were seen as symbols of conjugal happiness. Here, the poet wishes to prevent the swallows from reminding the lonely wife that her husband is out traveling and is not with her.

玉帶暫時華，
金釵非久飾。
張翁與鄭婆，
一去無消息。

HS 54

可憐好丈夫，
身體極稜稜。
春秋未三十，
才藝百般能。
金羈逐俠客，
玉饌集良朋。
唯有一般惡，
不傳無盡燈。

HS 55

桃花欲經夏，
風月催不待。
訪覓漢時人，
能無一箇在。
朝朝花遷落，
歲歲人移改。

Jade belts only flourish for a time,
And gold hairpins will not adorn you for long.
Gaffer Zhang and Goody Zheng—
Once they're gone, we'll hear no more of them.

HS 54

Charming, this fine and stalwart man,
His physical presence, how majestic!
Not yet thirty in his years,
Yet skilled in a hundred arts.
His golden bridle follows after wandering heroes;
His fine delicacies bring together good companions.
He only has one kind of fault—
He does not transmit the Inexhaustible Lamp.[1]

HS 55

Peach flowers would like to last out the summer,
But wind and moon urge them on without ceasing.
If you look for the people who lived in the Han,
Not a single one is alive today!
Every morning, the flowers age and fall;
Every year, the people shift and change.

---

1 The Inexhuastible Lamp is the Dharma of the Buddha.

今日揚塵處，
8 昔時為大海。

HS 56

我見東家女，
年可有十八。
西舍競來問，
4 願姻夫妻活。
烹羊煑眾命，
聚頭作婬殺。
含笑樂呵呵，
8 啼哭受殃抉。

HS 57

田舍多桑園，
牛犢滿廄轍。
肯信有因果，
4 頑皮早晚裂。
眼看消磨盡，
當頭各自活。
紙袴瓦作裩，
8 到頭凍餓殺。

The place where we drive up dust today
Was a great sea in the past.

HS 56

I see that girl from the family to the east;
She's seventeen years old or so.[1]
Houses to the west vie in courting her;
They want to marry, live as husband and wife.
Then they simmer a sheep, boil many living things;
Together they indulge in reckless slaughter.
All smiles, they laugh delightedly;
But they'll sob when they face calamitous tortures.[2]

HS 57

Their farmstead has many mulberry trees and gardens;
Oxen and calves fill its stables and paths.
Are they not willing to believe in karma?
When will their stubborn hides crack?
With their own eyes they'll see their things melt away,
Suddenly each will seek to preserve himself.
With paper trousers and pants fashioned of shards,
In the end they'll all die of cold and hunger.

1 "Eighteen" by traditional Chinese reckoning, where one is already one year old at birth and adds a year at every New Year.
2 They will be reborn in a Hell realm because they took animal life.

HS 58

我見百十狗，
箇箇毛鬇鬡。
臥者渠自臥，
行者渠自行。
投之一塊骨，
相與啀喍爭。
良由為骨少，
狗多分不平。

HS 59

極目兮長望，
白雲四茫茫。
鴟鴉飽腲腇，
鸞鳳飢徬徨。
駿馬放石磧，
蹇驢能至堂。
天高不可問，
鷦鵁在滄浪。

HS 58

I see over a hundred dogs,
Each ferocious, with bristling fur.
Some of them lie, content to lie;
Some walk, content to walk.
But throw a piece of bone to them:
Showing their fangs, they'll fight each other for it.
When the bones you have are just too few,
You can't be fair with so many dogs!

HS 59

As I gaze far, to my vision's end,
The white clouds rise, all about me welling.
Owl and crow sit plump and contented,
While simurgh and phoenix fly about in their hunger.
The swift horse is pastured on stony wastes,
While the lame ass can enter the hall.
High heaven will not hear your questions:
A wren is drifting on the waves.[1]

1 It is unclear what bird is meant by the noun *jiaojia* here. It is likely to be the same as the *jiaoliao* (wren) mentioned in HS 5. Regardless, the context suggests a small and insignificant bird.

HS 60

洛陽多女兒，
春日逞華麗。
共折路邊花，
各持插高髻。
髻高花匼匝，
人見皆睥睨。
別求醦醦憐，
將歸見夫婿。

HS 61

春女衒容儀，
相將南陌陲。
看花愁日晚，
隱樹怕風吹。
年少從傍來，
白馬黃金羈。
何須久相弄，
兒家夫婿知。

HS 60

Luoyang has many girls
Who show off their beauty on a spring day.
All of them pluck a roadside flower
And each takes it, inserting it in her high coiffure.
Coiffures high, and the flowers surround them—
When men see them, the girls give them the eye.
"Do not seek a useless love from us![1]
We're just going home to see our husbands."

HS 61

The girls of spring show off their stunning looks,
Go hand in hand along the south field lanes.
Sad that the day grows late in their flower-viewing,
They hide under trees, in fear of the wind.
A youth comes galloping up to them,
On a white horse with a golden bridle.
"Why must you stay there teasing us?
Our husbands back home will find out!"

---

1 This is somewhat speculative based on the context. *Chen* is another term for "vinegar," so *chenchen lian* literally means "sour affection."

HS 62

群女戲夕陽，
風來滿路香。
綴裙金蛺蝶，
插髻玉鴛鴦。
角婢紅羅縝，
閹奴紫錦裳。
為觀失道者，
鬢白心惶惶。

HS 63

若人逢鬼魅，
第一莫驚懅。
捺硬莫采渠，
呼名自當去。
燒香請佛力，
禮拜求僧助。
蚊子叮鐵牛，
無渠下觜處。

HS 62

A group of girls play in the setting sun:
When breezes come, they fill the road with their scent.
Their embroidered skirts are worked with golden butterflies;
Inserted in their coiffures are jade mandarin ducks.
Their pigtailed servants wear red silk aprons;
Their eunuch attendants have purple brocade robes.
They have come to observe one who has lost his way:
His temples graying, his heart in turmoil.

HS 63

If you should meet a mountain goblin,
The most important thing: do not panic.
Force yourself to ignore him;
And if you call him by name, he'll disappear.
Burning incense to request the Buddha's strength,
Doing obeisance in seeking aid from monks:
That's a mosquito biting into an iron ox—
No place for him to sink his teeth!

HS 64

浩浩黃河水，
東流長不息。
悠悠不見清，
人人壽有極。
苟欲乘白雲，
曷由生羽翼。
唯當鬒髮時，
行住須努力。

HS 65

乘茲朽木船，
采彼紝婆子。
行至大海中，
波濤復不止。
唯賚一宿糧，
去岸三千里。
煩惱從何生，
愁哉緣苦起。

HS 64

Surge upon surge, the Yellow River waters,
Flowing eastwards, never ceasing.
Though you gaze far, you won't find them clear;
And every human life has its limits.
If you wished to ride the white clouds,
How could you ever sprout wings?[1]
You should, while you're hair's still black,
Exert yourself in every moment![2]

HS 65

Riding a boat of rotting timbers,
And gathering the seeds of the neem tree,[3]
We travel out onto the wide sea,
Where the billows never cease.
Relying only on one day's provision,
We're a thousand miles from shore.
From where do these *kleśa* spring?[4]
Alas! They arise from karmic woe.

---

1 That is, wish to become immortal. Immortals could often take the form of cranes.

2 This poem could be suggesting that since the search for immortality is futile, one should make sure one's limited life is worthwhile (since this is a common poetic trope, that reading is more likely). If its attitude is Buddhist, it could also be stressing the importance of cultivating practice while one is still young.

3 The neem or neemb is an Indian tree that produces leaves, flowers, and fruit noted for their bitterness. A passage in the Nirvana Sutra compares the seeds to evil acts with evil karmic consequences—just as the bitter neem seeds produce a tree that is bitter in all of its parts.

4 *Kleśa* (*fannao*) are the factors that interfere with Buddhist practice and cause one to generate bad karma.

HS 66

默默永無言，
後生何所述。
隱居在林藪，
智日何由出。
枯槁非堅衛，
風霜成夭疾。
土牛耕石田，
未有得稻日。

HS 67

山中何太冷，
自古非今年。
沓嶂恆凝雪，
幽林每吐煙。
草生芒種後，
葉落立秋前。
此有沈迷客，
窺窺不見天。

HS 66

If you keep silent and never speak,
What can be told to later generations?
If you live as a recluse in forest thicket,
How can the sun of wisdom emerge?
Emaciation does not make you a steadfast guard;
Wind and frost will bring about early death.
If you use a clay ox to plow a stony field,
You'll never see a day for harvest.[1]

HS 67

How very cold it is in the mountains!
Always so—not just this year.
Piled-up cliffs are ever frozen in snow,
Remote forests are always emitting their mists.
Grass grows only after "Grain in Ear,"
And leaves will fall before "Autumn Rises."[2]
And here is a traveler, thoroughly lost,
Who squints and squints and can't see the sky.

1 Effigies of oxen fashioned out of clay sometimes were featured at agricultural festivals. Thus to attempt to employ such an ox for real farming became proverbial for doing something useless. See also SD 29.

2 These are two of the twenty-four solar terms that mark the agricultural calendar. "Grain in Ear" begins June 6; "Autumn Established" begins August 7.

HS 68

山客心悄悄，
常嗟歲序遷。
辛勤采芝朮，
披斥詎成仙。
庭廓雲初卷，
林明月正圓。
不歸何所為，
桂樹相留連。

HS 69a

有人坐山楹，
雲卷兮霞瓔。
秉芳兮欲寄，
路漫漫難征。
心惆悵狐疑，
年老已無成。
衆喔咿斯蹇，
獨立兮忠貞。

HS 68

The mountain dweller is troubled in heart,
Always sighing at the passing of the years.
So he labors hard to pick his mushrooms and thistles—[1]
But how can his choices make him immortal?
The courtyard is broad—the clouds are clearing;
The forest is bright—the moon is now full.
Why should I not go home now?
The cinnamon tree detains me.[2]

HS 69a[3]

There is a person sitting in a mountain lodge,
Where clouds roil about (oh!) and rose mists coil.
He holds a flower in his hand (oh!), he wants to send it,
But the road is far and the journey hard.
His heart grieves sore and he hesitates,
He grows old with years yet has accomplished naught.
The crowd laughs scornfully at his sad plight;
Yet he stands alone (oh!), is loyal and pure.

1 Traditionally mentioned as ingredients in elixirs of immortality.

2 A cinnamon tree is said to grow in the moon, so the poet is saying he that the beauty of the moonlight detains him. I believe it not unlikely that HS 68 is two quatrains that have been accidentally run together because of their shared rhyme.

3 HS 69 exists in a number of versions, possibly because it was originally composed in the meter and style characteristic of the *Chuci* collection (marked by the use of the metrical caesura particle 兮), and different editors of the collection were uncomfortable with it. 69a (the *Sibu congkan* version) shows some signs that someone attempted to revise a more eccentric poem to fit the 8-line pentasyllabic format—including removal of the *xi* particle in some lines and shifting characters to five-line forms (resulting in the awkward violation of poetic caesuras in lines four and five). I have included as 69b a more consistent version taken from other editions.

HS 69b

有人兮山陘，
雲卷兮霞纓。
秉芳兮欲寄，
路漫兮難征。
心惆悵兮狐疑，
蹇獨立兮忠貞。

HS 70

豬喫死人肉，
人喫死豬腸。
豬不嫌人臭，
人反道豬香。
豬死拋水內，
人死掘土藏。
彼此莫相噉，
蓮花生沸湯。

HS 69b

There is a person (oh!) in a mountain gorge,
Where clouds roil about (oh!) and rose mists coil.
He holds a flower in his hand (oh!) he wants to send it,
But the road is far (oh!) and the journey hard.
His heart grieves sore (oh!) he hesitates,
Yet he stands alone (oh!), is loyal and pure.

HS 70

Pigs eat the flesh of dead men;
People eat the innards of dead pigs.
Pigs do not abhor the stink of man;
And men, for their part, say pigs are fragrant.
When a pigs die, they'll throw them in the water;
When people die, they dig a hole and hide them away.
If both would just stop eating each other,
Lotus flowers would grow in boiling soup.

HS 71

快哉混沌身，
不飯復不尿。
遭得誰鑽鑿，
4 因茲立九竅。
朝朝為衣食，
歲歲愁租調。
千箇爭一錢，
8 聚頭亡命叫。

HS 72

啼哭緣何事，
淚如珠子顆。
應當有別離，
4 復是遭喪禍。
所為在貧窮，
未能了因果。
塚間瞻死屍，
8 六道不干我。

HS 71

How happy we were with undifferentiated selves!
We didn't eat, we didn't piss.
Then we encountered somebody who drilled away,
And so we got these nine holes.[1]
Now every day we work for clothes and food,
And every year we deplore our taxes.
And a thousand will fight over a single copper,
Shouting together with all their might.

HS 72

Why are you all sobbing like that,
With your falling tears like pearls?
You ought to know there is separation;
And you'll encounter loss and misfortune too.
What you do comes from your poverty,
And you have yet to understand karmic laws.
I contemplate the corpses amid the grave mounds,
And the Six Paths have no effect on me.[2]

---

1 This is an allusion to a passage in the *Zhuangzi*, in which the gods of the North and South provide the god Undifferentiated (*hundun*) with the holes he supposedly needs to see, hear, and eat (the so-called seven holes of the human head: ears, eyes, nostrils, and mouth). After they finish their operation, Undifferentiated dies. Zhuangzi uses it as a parable of the evils of distinction and differentiation in human society; the poet here sees it as a symbol for suffering in the samsaric world—the "holes" are the passages through which sensual awareness reaches our consciousness. He also adds two holes, as in some Chinese lists: the urethra or vaginal opening and the anus.

2 The Six Paths are the six realms of possible rebirth in samsara: Hell, hungry ghosts, animals, humans, angry gods, and gods. The poet here is engaging in a form of meditation in which the practitioner observes the decay of human bodies in order to break attachment to the flesh.

HS 73

婦人慵經織，
男夫懶耨田。
輕浮耽挾彈，
4 跕躧拈抹弦。
凍骨衣應急，
充腸食在先。
今誰念於汝，
8 苦痛哭蒼天。

HS 74

不行真正道，
隨邪號行婆。
口慙神佛少，
4 心懷嫉妒多。
背後噇魚肉，
人前念佛陀。
如此修身處，
8 難應避柰河。

HS 73

Wives grown indolent at wheel and loom!
Husbands too lazy to weed your fields!
You lightly play with your slings and darts,
Shuffle your slippers and twang your lutes.
When bones are chilled, then clothes are a must;
If you want a full belly, food should come first.
For who now is concerned for you,
In your bitter pain as you sob to the blue skies?

HS 74

They don't practice the Way of True and Right,
But follow the wicked—these "practicing grannies."
Seldom their mouths give thanks to gods or Buddhas,
While their hearts often dwell on jealousy.
Behind others' backs they chew fish and flesh,
While they chant the Buddha's name in public.
With this way of "cultivating the self"
They'll never escape the Hopeless River.[1]

1 *Nai he*, an expression that means "there is nothing you can do," is used as a pun to name a river of Hell that all souls must cross on their way to judgment and rebirth. See also HS 237.

HS 75

世有一等愚，
茫茫恰似驢。
還解人言語，
貪婬狀若豬。
險巇難可測，
實語却成虛。
誰能共伊語，
令教莫此居。

HS 76

有漢姓傲慢，
名貪字不廉。
一身無所解，
百事被他嫌。
死惡黃連苦，
生憐白蜜甜。
喫魚猶未止，
食肉更無猒。

HS 75

There's a kind of fool in the world,
Muddle-headed, exactly like an ass.
He may understand what you have to say,
But he's porcine in his greed and lust.
He's a deep one—you can't fathom him,
And his "words of truth" will turn to falsehood.
Who can have a word with him
And convince him to not live here?

HS 76

There's a man with the surname "Haughty,"
"Greedy" his name, "Corrupted" his style.[1]
His whole body a mass of ignorance,
Others doubtful about everything he does.
Death he loathes, as bitter as goldthread;[2]
Life he loves, as sweet as white honey.
He still hasn't stopped eating his fish,
Nor is he surfeited on flesh.

1 "Style" (*zi*) indicates the individual's formal name, used by others out of courtesy.
2 Goldthread (*huanglian*) is a plant (coptis chinensis) whose bitter root is used in traditional medicine.

HS 77

縱你居犀角，
饒君帶虎睛。
桃枝將辟穢，
4 蒜殼取為瓔。
暖腹茱萸酒，
空心枸杞羹。
終歸不免死，
8 浪自覓長生。

HS 78

卜擇幽居地，
天台更莫言。
猨啼谿霧冷，
4 嶽色草門連。
折葉覆松室，
開池引澗泉。
已甘休萬事，
8 采蕨度殘年。

HS 77

Suppose that you live with a rhino horn,
And use tiger-eyes for your sash;
Use peach tree branches to ward off pollution,
Fashion a necklace of garlic bulbs;
Warm your bellies with prickly-ash wine,
Clear your minds with goji berry porridge.[1]
In the end you'll return; you can't avoid death.
In vain is your search for long life.

HS 78

I found a plot for my home in a remote place—
Tiantai—what more need be said?
Gibbons cry, their sound chill in the valley mist.
The color of the peaks reaches my weedy gate.
I pluck leaves to thatch my home in the pines,
Dig a pool, channel the stream water there.
Already content to give up all affairs,
I'll pass my last years gathering mountain greens.

---

1 This poem mentions a variety of remedies and talismans meant to protect the life and longevity of the wearer/consumer.

HS 79

益者益其精，
可名為有益。
易者易其形，
是名之有易。
能益復能易，
當得上仙籍。
無益復無易，
終不免死厄。

HS 80

徒勞說三史，
浪自看五經。
洎老檢黃籍，
依前注白丁。
筮遭連蹇卦，
生主虛危星。
不及河邊樹，
年年一度青。

HS 79

By "benefit," I mean "benefit one's essence";
This could be called "beneficial."
By "change" I mean "change one's form";
This is termed "changeable."
If you can benefit, if you can change,
Then you'll be placed on the roster of Transcendents;
But with no benefit and no change,
You'll never escape the calamity of death.[1]

HS 80

Vain to toil in reading the Three Histories;[2]
A waste to peruse the Five Classics.
I'll be listed in tax rolls until I'm old,
Always registered as a commoner.[3]
Casting my fate, always "obstruction" comes up;[4]
A life ever governed by the "barren" and "danger" stars.[5]
It would be better to be a riverside tree,
That gets to turn green once every year.

1 This very Daoist poem is a versification of a passage from "The Private History of Emperor Wu of the Han" (*Han Wudi nei zhuan* 漢武帝內傳), in which the Queen Mother of the West explains to the emperor the secrets of longevity.

2 These are the first three of the official histories: *Shi ji*, *Han Shu*, *Hou Han shu*.

3 That is, no matter how hard the speaker studies, he will never pass the examinations and will always keep his commoner status.

4 A reference to hexagram #39 in the *Yijing*: *jian* or "obstruction".

5 *Xu* ("barrens") and *wei* ("danger") are two of the twenty-four asterisms that are used in Chinese astrology. They govern disaster and loss.

HS 81

碧澗泉水清，
寒山月華白。
默知神自明，
觀空境逾寂。

HS 82

我今有一襦，
非羅復非綺。
借問作何色，
不紅亦不紫。
夏天將作衫，
冬天將作被。
冬夏遞互用，
長年只這是。

HS 83

白拂栴檀柄，
馨香竟日聞。
柔和如卷霧，
搖拽似行雲。

HS 81

Clear stream water in the emerald dale;
Moonlight white on Cold Mountain.
In the silence, I know Spirit is itself bright;
I look into Emptiness: realms ever more quiet.

HS 82

Today I have a jacket,
Not fashioned of gauze or patterned silk.
You may ask what color it is—
4 It's not crimson, nor is it purple.
In summer it makes do for a shirt,
In winter it makes do for a coverlet.
Winter and summer, I switch its uses—
8 Through my long life I only have this.

HS 83

A white fly-whisk, with sandalwood handle;[1]
One can smell its fragrance throughout the day.
Gentle it is, like billowing mist,
4 Wafting gently, like moving clouds.

1 Fly whisks were commonly used by abbots and other authority figures in the Buddhist church as an aid to rhetorical gestures in their sermons and conversations.

禮奉宜當暑，
高提復去塵。
時時方丈內，
將用指迷人。

HS 84

貪愛有人求快活，
不知禍在百年身。
但看陽燄浮漚水，
便覺無常敗壞人。
丈夫志氣直如鐵，
無曲心中道自真。
行密節高霜下竹，
方知不枉用心神。

HS 85

多少般數人，
百計求名利。
心貪覓榮華，
經營圖富貴。

Offered politely, it's good for dealing with the heat;
Raised aloft, it can remove dust too.
And sometimes, within the abbot's cell,
8 It's used to point the way for those who are lost.

HS 84

Greedy and covetous, there are people who seek for happiness,
Unaware that disaster resides within their mortal bodies.
Just look at a single flame that floats upon the froth;
4 Then you'll realize how Impermanence defeats and ruins us.
An upright man's willful force is as straight as iron;
And through his never-crooked mind the way is naturally true.
Dense in growth with lofty joints, that bamboo under the frost:[1]
8 We can know then that it's not a waste to exert the mind and spirit.

HS 85

So many different kinds of men:
With many schemes they seek fame and profit.
Their minds are greedy as they seek their glory,
4 Laying plans, plotting for wealth and status.

1 Because of bamboo's ability to withstand cold weather, it became a symbol for thriving under adversity. Here there are other plays on words as well: "dense in growth" could mean "careful in conduct," and "lofty joints" could mean "lofty self-restraint."

心未片時歇，
奔突如煙氣。
家眷實團圓，
8 一呼百諾至。
不過七十年，
冰消瓦解置。
死了萬事休，
12 誰人承後嗣。
水浸泥彈丸，
方知無意智。

HS 86

貪人好聚財，
恰如梟愛子。
子大而食母，
4 財多還害己。
散之即福生，
聚之即禍起。
無財亦無禍，
8 鼓翼青雲裏。

Their minds never have a moment's rest,
Rushing about like a surging fog.
A large family's truly all around them;
A hundred assents to every summons.
But seventy years have not passed by
When the ice melts away and the tiles will shatter.
He'll die, and all earthly affairs will end;
Who then will stand to inherit?
It's like water soaking a ball of mud—
You'll know then there's no wisdom in it.

HS 86

Greedy people who like to hoard wealth
Are just like the owls who love their chicks.
When the chick gets big it eats its mother;
When wealth is great it will harm you.
Get rid of it, then good fortune is born;
Collect it and disaster arises.
No wealth, and then no disaster—
You can beat your wings amid the blue clouds.

HS 87

去家一萬里，
提劍擊匈奴。
得利渠即死，
失利汝即殂。
渠命既不惜，
汝命有何辜。
教汝百勝術，
不貪為上謨。

HS 88

嗔是心中火，
能燒功德林。
欲行菩薩道，
忍辱護真心。

HS 87

You're away from home ten thousand leagues,
Drawing your sword to strike the Xiongnu.[1]
If you get the advantage, then *he* will die;
If you lose it, *you* will perish.
Since you don't care if he lives or dies,
What guilt does your own life bear?
I'll teach you the art of a hundred victories:
Not coveting is the best plan of all.

HS 88

Anger is a fire in the mind
That can burn down your forest of merit.
If you wish to travel the Bodhisattva's path,
Forbear, and protect your true mind.

1 The Xiongnu were northern nomads frequently involved in border wars during the Han dynasty. After the Han, they became a standard literary term for enemy peoples to the north, particularly in frontier poetry.

HS 89

汝為埋頭癡兀兀，
愛向無明羅刹窟。
再三勸你早修行，
是你頑癡心恍惚。
不肯信受寒山語，
轉轉倍加業汨汨。
直待斬首作兩段，
方知自身奴賊物。

HS 90

惡趣甚茫茫，
冥冥無日光。
人間八百歲，
未抵半宵長。
此等諸癡子，
論情甚可傷。
勸君求出離，
認取法中王。

HS 89

All of you bury your heads away, foolish and muddle-headed.
You love to seek the cavern of the demon Ignorance.
Over and over, I've urged you to start your practice early;
It's you who are dim and stupid, your minds lost in a daze.
You're unwilling to put your trust in Cold Mountain's words;
More and more, ever increasing, your evil karma flows on.
Just wait until your head's cut off and you are split in two;
Then you'll know that your own Self is just a slave, a bandit.

HS 90

How limitless the Three Evil Paths;[1]
Murky and dark without a sun.
Eight hundred years of human life
Don't fill out half a night-time there.
All the fools of this type
To tell the truth, are really pathetic.
I urge you sir, to seek release,
And acknowledge the Prince of the Dharma.[2]

---

1 The three unfortunate paths of rebirth: animals, hungry ghosts, and the Hell realms.

2 The Buddha.

HS 91

世有多解人，
愚癡徒苦辛。
不求當來善，
4 唯知造惡因。
五逆十惡輩，
三毒以為親。
一死入地獄，
8 長如鎮庫銀。

HS 92

天高高不窮，
地厚厚無極。
動物在其中，
4 憑茲造化力。
爭頭覓飽暖，
作計相噉食。
因果都未詳，
8 盲兒問乳色。

HS 91

In the world there are men with "great understanding"
Who are foolish—only suffer and toil.
They don't seek the good of their future lives;
Only know how to create evil karma.
The Five Perversions, the Ten Evil Acts,
The Three Poisons they take as kin.[1]
And once they die, they enter Hell,
Held there as long as good-luck silver.[2]

HS 92

The Heavens are high—high and forever;
The Earth is deep—deep and endless.
Living things dwell between them,
And rely on them to produce transformations.
They vie in seeking contentment and warmth,
Lay plans to devour each other.
Of causes and results they understand little:
Blind men asking about the color of milk.

1 The Five Perversions are: Killing one's father, killing one's mother, killing an arhat, destroying the harmony of the sangha, and shedding the blood of a Buddha. The Ten Evil Acts are: killing, robbery, illicit sex, wild speech, lying, slander, flattery, greed, anger, and perverse views. The Three Poisons are greed, anger, and ignorance.

2 Silver kept in one's warehouse permanently for emergencies; such silver was also thought to suppress bad luck and preserve good fortune. The term literally means "suppression warehouse silver."

HS 93

天下幾種人，
論時色數有。
賈婆如許夫，
4 黃老元無婦。
衛氏兒可憐，
鐘家女極醜。
渠若向西行，
8 我便東邊走。

HS 94

賢士不貪婪，
癡人好鑪冶。
麥地占他家，
4 竹園皆我者。
努膊覓錢財，
切齒驅奴馬。
須看郭門外，
8 壘壘松柏下。

HS 93

The various kinds of people in the world,
To tell the truth, have their different aspects.
Old lady Jia had so many husbands,
While Old Huang never had a wife at all.
The Wei clan's boy was quite charming,
While the Zhong family girl was ugly indeed.
If *he* decides to head off to the west,
Then *I* will run to the east.[1]

HS 94

A worthy gentleman controls his greed,
While the fool is fond of his alchemy.[2]
He'll occupy the fields of others,
Claim bamboo and gardens as his own.
Flexing his arms, he seeks out wealth;
Grinding his teeth, he drives a worn-out nag.
He should look beyond the city walls,
At the mounds piled up below pine and cypress.[3]

---

1 This poem simply emphasizes the arbitrary aspects and tastes of human beings. Commentators spend much energy linking each of the four people mentioned in lines 3–6 with specific historical actors, with greater or less plausibility; but I suspect the author is mostly using each surname in the manner of a "Mr. Smith" or a "Miss Jones." The last couplet should not be taken as the author's preference, but simply as another example of human perversity—if someone does one thing, someone else is bound to do the opposite.

2 I.e., experiments in creating gold.

3 Grave mounds.

HS 95

嗔嗔買魚肉，
擔歸餧妻子。
何須殺他命，
4 將來活汝己。
此非天堂緣，
純是地獄滓。
徐六語破堆，
8 始知沒道理。

HS 96

有人把椿樹，
喚作白栴檀。
學道多沙數，
4 幾箇得泥丸。
棄金却擔草，
謾他亦自謾。
似聚砂一處，
8 成團也大難。

HS 95

"Mid shouting and bustle you buy fish and flesh,
And bear it back home to feed wife and child.
But why must you take the life of another
And use it to sustain your own existence?
Those aren't conditions that lead to Heaven;
They're purely the dregs of Hell."
The words of Xu Six have hit the mark,
You'll know then that this makes no sense.[1]

HS 96

There are people who would call the ailanthus[2]
By the name of white sandalwood.
There are many who study the Dharma,
But only a few who will find nirvana.
They'll cast away gold and carry weeds instead,
Deceiving others and deceiving themselves.
Like piling up sand in one place—
You can't make it form a ball.

1 The identity of Xu Six is not known. It may just be another one of Hanshan's hypothetical speakers. Here he lectures the poem's persona on vegetarianism.

2 A tree known not just for its unpleasant odor but for the uselessness of its wood.

HS 97

蒸砂擬作飯,
臨渴始掘井。
用力磨碌甎,
那堪將作鏡。
佛說平元等,
總有真如性。
但自審思量,
不用閑爭競。

HS 98

推尋世間事,
子細總皆知。
凡事莫容易,
盡愛討便宜。
護即弊成好,
毀即是成非。
故知雜濫口,
背面總由伊。
冷暖我自量,
不信奴脣皮。

HS 97

Steam sand, planning to make rice—
Digging a well only when you thirst.
Use your strength to polish a piece of tile—
When will it ever become a mirror?[1]
The Buddha's words hold all things equal,
Always possess the nature of True Suchness.[2]
If you really think carefully about it,
It's useless to vie and struggle.

HS 98

Examine the affairs of this world:
Carefully, so you know all:
Common affairs are hardly easy;
All love to seek what they prefer.
In defense they'll turn the bad to good,
In slander they'll turn what is true to false.
So you know that those who endlessly debate
Are just secretly choosing what they want.
I'll judge the hot and the cold for myself:
In this I won't trust what those guys say.

1 A proverbial expression for useless effort in seeking enlightenment—most famously expressed in a story in which the early Chan master Mazu Daoyi 馬祖道一 persuades Nanyue Huairang 南嶽懷讓 that meditation is like polishing a tile to create a mirror.

2 "All things equal" explains the Sanskrit term *samatā*, which can mean equanimity as well, the ability to not cling to things. True Suchness (*zhenru*) is *bhūtatathatā*, a Mahayana term used to express ultimate reality.

HS 99

蹭蹬諸貧士，
飢寒成至極。
閑居好作詩，
札札用心力。
賤他言孰采，
勸君休歎息。
題安糊餅上，
乞狗也不喫。

HS 100

欲識生死譬，
且將冰水比。
水結即成冰，
冰消返成水。
已死必應生，
出生還復死。
冰水不相傷，
生死還雙美。

HS 99

Stumbling along, those poor scholars,
Their hunger and cold have reached the extreme.
In their idleness they like to write verse,
Toiling away, using all their brains.
They're low-ranking, so who will prefer their words?
But I urge them not to sigh about it.
If you were to write your verse on a cake,
A dog wouldn't eat it if you asked him.[1]

HS 100

Would you know a likeness for life and death?
Then try comparing water to ice.
Water freezes and turns to ice;
Ice melts and returns to water.
Already dead; you'll live again.
Another life; you'll die once more.
Ice and water won't harm each other:
Life and death are a paired delight.

1 Or "even a begging dog wouldn't eat it."

HS 101

尋思少年日，
遊獵向平陵。
國使職非願，
神仙未足稱。
聯翩騎白馬，
喝兔放蒼鷹。
不覺大流落，
皤皤誰見矜。

HS 102

偃息深林下，
從生是農夫。
立身既質直，
出語無諂諛。
保我不鑒璧，
信君方得珠。
焉能同泛灩，
極目波上鳧。

HS 101

I think back on the days of my youth,
When I'd go hunting toward Pingling.[1]
A position as state courier was not my wish,
And I never thought the Transcendent Way worth praising.
I galloped about upon my white steed,
Called out hares, let loose my gray hawk.
Then unawares, I went into a great decline:
White-haired, who is concerned for me?

HS 102

I hid away in a deep wood,
Taking up life as a farmer.
I established myself as upright and straight,
Never uttered flattery or slander.
I protect my unexamined jade,[2]
I'll leave it to you to find the pearl.[3]
How can I join them in the drift and flow?
At the edge of my sight, those ducks on the waves.

---

1 A fashionable suburb of the capital in Han times; later, it was used in poetry to describe neighborhoods of the elites.

2 Probably a reference to the famous piece of jade discovered by Mr. He 和氏 in the Warring States period. He attempted to persuade different rulers of its value, but instead found himself brutally punished. Finally the value of the jade was discovered and was fashioned into a precious disk. Since then, the story has become a metaphor for unrecognized talents. Here, the speaker says he prefers to live as a recluse rather than seek office.

3 I take this to refer to the active desire to attain office or status. Various commentators find specific allusions here, but none strike me as satisfactory.

HS 103

不須攻人惡，
何用伐己善。
行之則可行，
卷之則可卷。
祿厚憂積大，
言深慮交淺。
聞茲若念茲，
小子當自見。

HS 104

富兒會高堂，
華燈何煒煌。
此時無燭者，
心願處其傍。
不意遭排遣，
還歸暗處藏。
益人明詎損，
頓訝惜餘光。

HS 103

No need to attack the other's faults;
And what use to flaunt your own virtues?
If you're going to take action then go ahead;
If you're going to withdraw, then do that too.
Salary generous—worry about your great duties;[1]
Advice profound—fret that your connections are weak.
Hear this, all of you, and remember!
You young ones will discover this for yourselves.

HS 104

Wealthy lads assemble in the high hall;
Their fancy lanterns—how bright they shine!
Just then, a man without a candle
Wants to stay at their side.
You wouldn't think he'd be refused, ejected,
Sent home to dwell alone in darkness.
How is it less bright when light is shared with others?
How surprising—they begrudged their extra light.

1 I accept that the correct character for 積 ("accumulate") here should be 責 ("duty"), in keeping with other editions.

HS 105

世有聰明士，
勤苦探幽文。
三端自孤立，
六藝越諸君。
神氣卓然異，
精彩超眾群。
不識箇中意，
逐境亂紛紛。

HS 106

層層山水秀，
煙霞鎖翠微。
嵐拂紗巾濕，
露霑簑草衣。
足躡遊方履，
手執古藤枝。
更觀塵世外，
夢境復何為。

HS 105

There are clever scholars in the world,
Who toil way, plunged in writings obscure.
They stand alone with their Three Tips,[1]
Surpass all others in the Six Arts.[2]
The force of their spirit is manifestly unique,
Their brilliance goes beyond the common crowd.
But they don't know the Central Import,[3]
And bustle about the world in frenzied disorder.

HS 106

Scene upon scene, the landscape superb;
Mist and rosy clouds enclose the distant mountain green.
Fog brushes and dampens my silken head cloth;
The dew soaks my raincoat made of straw.
My feet tread in wanderer's shoes,
My hand grasps an old rattan staff.
If you look beyond this dusty world,
What is there other than a realm of dreams?

---

1 The "three tips" (brush, weapon, and tongue) are skills in writing, marital arts, and oratory.

2 The traditional six arts of early Confucianism are: rites, music, archery, charioteering, calligraphy, and arithmetic.

3 That is, the Buddhist dharma.

HS 107

滿卷才子詩，
溢壺聖人酒。
行愛觀牛犢，
4 坐不離左右。
霜露入茅簷，
月華明瓮牖。
此時吸兩甌，
8 吟詩五百首。

HS 108

施家有兩兒，
以藝干齊楚。
文武各自備，
4 託身為得所。
孟公問其術，
我子親教汝。
秦衛兩不成，
8 失時成齟齬。

HS 107

Filling the scroll, a talented man's verse;
Filling the jug, wine of the Sage.[1]
When walking, I love to go see my oxen and calves;
When I sit, scroll and jug never leave my side.
Frost and dew penetrate my thatched eaves;
Moonlight brightens my ramshackle window.[2]
Now is when I'll sip a few cups,
And chant five hundred poems!

HS 108

The Shi family had two sons,
Who with their skills sought jobs in Qi and Chu.
One was versed in civil, the other, martial affairs;
So they committed themselves and found a place.
Master Meng asked after their method;
"My sons will tell you themselves:
Your sons both failed in Qin and Wei;
Their timing was bad, and so nothing went right."[3]

---

1 Wine of the Sage was a clear, strained wine, as opposed to Wine of the Worthy, which was muddy and considered of lower quality.

2 Literally, "jug-window," a window frame formed from a broken jug—a poetic cliché for a rustic dwelling.

3 This is a versification of an anecdote from the *Liezi*. One of the sons of Mr. Shi found a job as a Confucian tutor in Qi; another found a job as a military strategist in Chu. When Mr. Meng's sons attempted the same thing, they picked the wrong countries: one attempted to find a tutor job in the militaristic Qin, the other a strategist position in the weak and accommodating Wei. As a result, one son was castrated, and the other had his feet cut off.

HS 109

止宿鴛鴦鳥，
一雄兼一雌。
銜花相共食，
刷羽每相隨。
戲入煙霄裏，
宿歸沙岸湄。
自憐生處樂，
不奪鳳皇池。

HS 110

或有衒行人，
才藝過周孔。
見罷頭兀兀，
看時身侗侗。
繩牽未肯行，
錐刺猶不動。
恰似羊公鶴，
可憐生氃氋。

HS 109

Stopping to roost, a pair of mandarin ducks:
One of them male, the other female.
Blossoms in beaks, they feed one another;
Scrubbing their feathers, they travel together.
Playfully they enter the misty vault above;
When roosting, they return to their sandy bank.
They naturally love their place of birth:
They'll not seize a place at Phoenix Pool.[1]

HS 110

There's a man who boasts of his actions,
More talented than the Duke of Zhou or Confucius!
Just to see him will make you dizzy;
When you look at him, he seems splendid and grand.
Try leading him with a rope and he'll never budge;
Stick him with an awl and he won't jump at all.
He's just like those cranes of Master Yang:
How adorable they are as they shake their feathers![2]

---

1 Phoenix Pool can be a symbol for high political office.

2 Master Yang's cranes were trained to perform a dance, but when he invited some guests to watch them perform, they would simply stand and shake their feathers. The anecdote is applied to men who may seem impressive and talented but accomplish nothing.

HS 111

少小帶經鋤,
本將兄共居。
緣遭他輩責,
剩被自妻疎。
拋絕紅塵境,
常遊好閱書。
誰能借斗水,
活取轍中魚。

HS 112

變化計無窮,
生死竟不止。
三途鳥雀身,
五嶽龍魚已。
世濁作羱羺,
時清為騄駬。
前迴是富兒,
今度成貧士。

HS 111

When young I'd take along a book as I plowed,[1]
Back when I lived with my older brother.
Then because I met blame from others,
Even my wife kept her distance from me.
Let me cast aside this world of red dust,
Always go wandering with the books that I love!
Who can borrow a pail of water
And keep the cart-rut fish alive?[2]

HS 112

There's no end to Transformation's plans;
No stopping the cycles of life and death.
You're in the body of a bird on the Three Evil Paths,
Then a dragon or fish among the Five Peaks.
When the age is corrupt, you're a curly-fleeced ram,
When the times are fair, you're a fine, swift horse.[3]
Last time you were a wealthy young man;
Now you've become an impoverished scholar.

1 The text says "classic," but that term can apply to scriptures of all the major faiths. Probably standard Confucian texts are meant.
2 An anecdote from the *Zhuangzi* tells of a magical fish who was trapped in a cart-rut filled with water. When he begs Zhuangzi for some water, Zhuangzi tells him he'll get the king to divert a whole river for him. The fish replies that by then it will be too late.
3 Literally, "Green Ears," a famous steed that exemplifies a fine horse.

HS 113

書判全非弱，
嫌身不得官。
銓曹被拗折，
洗垢覓瘡瘢。
必也關天命，
今冬更試看。
盲兒射雀目，
偶中亦非難。

HS 114

貧驢欠一尺，
富狗剩三寸。
若分貧不平，
中半富與困。
始取驢飽足，
却令狗飢頓。
為汝熟思量，
令我也愁悶。

HS 113

I wasn't weak at all in Calligraphy or Judgments;
But they disliked my stature, so I didn't get a post.[1]
The Examination Board really grilled me;
They washed away dirt to look for my scars.[2]
But if this depends on Heaven's will,
This winter I'll try again and see.
When a blind man shoots for the sparrow's eye,
It's not impossible he'll hit it sometimes.

HS 114

An impoverished ass is short by a foot,
A wealthy dog has three inches too much.
If you give to the poor to correct the injustice,
In the process the wealthy will suffer.
If you start by making the ass satisfied,
It'll end by starving the dog.
If I think long on this for your sake,
It really makes me depressed.

1 In the Tang examination system, examinees were evaluated not just for their compositional skills, but for factors like neatness of handwriting and physical stature.
2 Proverbial for being excessive in fault-finding.

HS 115

柳郎八十二，
藍嫂一十八。
夫妻共百年，
相憐情狡猾。
弄璋字烏鹿，
擲瓦名婠妠。
屢見枯楊荑，
常遭青女殺。

HS 116

大有飢寒客，
生將獸魚殊。
長存磨石下，
時哭路邊隅。
累日空思飯，
經冬不識襦。
唯齎一束草，
并帶五升麩。

HS 115

"Young Master" Liu is eighty-two;
"Matron" Lan is but eighteen.
Husband and wife share a hundred years;[1]
They cherish each other, but their love's a deceit.
Their son played with seals; he was styled Tiger;
Their daughter toyed with tiles; she was named Sissy.[2]
But I've often seen shoots grow on withered willows;
Always the frost goddess kills them.[3]

HS 116

There are many cold and hungry men
Who by birth are different from beast and fish;
Yet they always shelter under millstones,
And often weep by the side of the road.
For many days they've thought of food in vain;
They pass the whole winter unaware of shirts.
They have for bedding but a bundle of straw,
And carry with them five pints of bran.

1 A sarcasm based on a popular blessing: "May husband and wife share a hundred years" (i.e., live a hundred years together). Here, the combined ages of the couple equal one hundred.

2 This couplet alludes to a *Shijing* poem that stresses the difference in the treatment of baby boys and baby girls; the boys are treated well and given fine seals to play with; the girls are treated poorly and can only play with earthen tiles. The names given the children are meant to be cute baby names with traditional gender associations.

3 In general, this poem is a satire on elderly men remarrying young women; the last couplet suggests that any offspring born of such a union will die young.

HS 117

赫赫誰壚肆，
其酒甚濃厚。
可憐高幡幟，
極目平升斗。
何意訝不售，
其家多猛狗。
童子欲來沽，
狗齩便是走。

HS 118

吁嗟濁濫處，
羅剎共賢人。
謂是等流類，
焉知道不親。
狐假師子勢，
詐妄却稱珍。
鉛礦入鑪冶，
方知金不真。

HS 117

Who owns that glittering wine shop there?
Its wine is dark and thick enough,
It has a lovely, lofty sign,
And the clerks are keen to measure fair.
Surprisingly, their sales are poor!
They have too many vicious dogs.
When serving lads stop in to buy,
The dogs will bite and the lads will flee.

HS 118

Alas, this place of pollution,
Where demons mingle with worthies.
But everyone thinks they're just the same,
So how could you know that their paths diverge?
Foxes ape the manner of lions,
Deceptions are praised as precious.
But put the lead ore in the furnace,
Then you'll know that their "gold" is fake.

HS 119

田家避暑月，
斗酒共誰歡。
雜雜排山果，
4 疎疎圍酒樽。
蘆莦將代席，
蕉葉且充盤。
醉後搘頤坐，
8 須彌小彈丸。

HS 120

箇是何措大，
時來省南院。
年可三十餘，
4 曾經四五選。
囊裏無青蚨，
篋中有黃卷。
行到食店前，
8 不敢暫迴面。

HS 119

In a farmer's house, avoiding the summer heat;
With whom should I share my drinking bouts?
Randomly I set out mountain fruit,
And scatter wine cups all about us.
Reeds are woven to serve as mats,
And plantain leaves replace our plates.
When we're drunk we'll sit, our chins on our hands,
And pretend that Sumeru's a little ball![1]

HS 120

What poor bookworm is this?
Sometimes he comes to the South Court exams.[2]
He's probably over thirty years old,
And has taken the test four or five times.
His purse is empty of "blue beetles";[3]
His satchel is filled with yellow scrolls.[4]
When he walks in front of the food shops,
He doesn't dare turn his head for a moment.[5]

1 In Buddhist cosmology, Mt. Sumeru is the large mountain situated in the center of every individual cosmos.
2 A court established by the Board of Rites in Tang times where the examinations were announced.
3 "Blue beetle": a slang term for copper cash.
4 Tang manuscripts were usually copied on paper with a yellow tint.
5 That is, to show that he is interested in food (and thus admit his own poverty).

HS 121

為人常喫用，
愛意須慳惜。
老去不自由，
漸被他推斥。
送向荒山頭，
一生願虛擲。
亡羊罷補穿，
失意終無極。

HS 122

浪造凌霄閣，
虛登百尺樓。
養生仍夭命，
誘讀詎封侯。
不用從黃口，
何須厭白頭。
未能端似箭，
且莫曲如鈎。

HS 121

People always have their cost of living;
Their covetous minds must learn parsimony.
Then they grow old, never at liberty,
4 Gradually pushed aside by others.
Sent off to a grave on an overgrown hill,
All the hopes of their lives are thrown away.
When the sheep's fled, give up blocking the holes;
8 There's no end to the disappointment.

HS 122

Useless to reach a lodge that pierces the sky,
Vain to climb a hundred-foot tower.
You'll nourish your life and still die young;
4 Be lured to study, but never be enfeoffed.
No good to imitate fledglings;[1]
Why be bothered by growing old?
If you can't be as straight as an arrow,
8 At least don't be as bent as a hook.

1 An allusion to a story in which Confucius finds out from a bird-catcher that fledglings are easier to catch than adult birds, because they are naïve and more greedy for food. Here, it suggests that a wise person should not imitate the petty or the immature.

HS 123

雲山疊疊連天碧，
路僻林深無客遊。
遠望孤蟾明皎皎，
近聞群鳥語啾啾。
老夫獨坐棲青嶂，
少室閑居任白頭。
可歎往年與今日，
無心還似水東流。

HS 124

富貴疎親聚，
只為多錢米。
貧賤骨肉離，
非關少兄弟。
急須歸去來，
招賢閣未啟。
浪行朱雀街，
踏破皮鞋底。

HS 123

Cloudy mountains, range on range, stretch their emerald to the sky;
Road remote, forest deep: no travelers wander here.
Afar I gaze at the solitary toad, bright and gleaming white;[1]
Nearby I hear the flocks of birds that twitter noisily.
An old man sits all alone, nesting on green cliffs;
Living idly in a little room, giving in to his old age.[2]
What's amazing: from former years up until today,
I've kept myself free of intentions, like water flowing east.

HS 124

Far relations flock to the wealthy and great;
It's only because of their money and grain.
Close kin will shun the poor and base;
It's not because they have few brothers.
You should go back home again,
For Summon-Worthy Lodge will never open.
It's vain to tread Vermillion Bird Street,
Wearing out the soles of your shoes.[3]

---

1 In traditional Chinese lore, a toad is said to dwell on the moon; this led to using "toad" as an elegant substitution.

2 I take the text's 少室 for 小室. Possibly the "small room ten foot square" of Vimalakirtī (and which later became a description of the abbot's residence—see HS 83) is meant here.

3 This poem condemns the power structure, suggesting that it is rooted entirely in relationships and wealthy connections. It would be better to be content at home, rather than seek public office by haunting the streets of the city. The Summon-Worthy Lodge was constructed by a Han prince to encourage talented men to join his entourage. Vermilion Bird Street was a major street in the Tang capital of Chang'an.

HS 125

我見一癡漢，
仍居三兩婦。
養得八九兒，
總是隨宜手。
丁防是新差，
資財非舊有。
黃蘗作驢鞦，
始知苦在後。

HS 126

新穀尚未熟，
舊穀今已無。
就貸一斗許，
門外立踟躕。
夫出教問婦，
婦出遣問夫。
慳惜不救乏，
財多為累愚。

HS 125

I have seen a foolish man
Who has two or three wives at home.
And he's raised eight or nine sons,
All of them obedient to his will.
But there's been a new round of army conscriptions,
And his wealth isn't what it was.[1]
Tie Amur cork bark to the crupper of your ass,
Then you'll know that the bitter comes from behind.[2]

HS 126

The new grain has yet to ripen,
While the old grain's already run out.
So I go to borrow a measure or so,
Hesitating outside of their gate.
The husband comes out, tells me to ask the wife;
The wife comes out, sends me to ask the husband.
Being stingy won't save those who lack;
When your wealth is great, you're even more stupid.

1 The man will not be able to buy exemptions from conscription for his sons.
2 The wood of the Amur cork tree had a medicinal bark with a bitter taste. The proverbial image here is that nothing lasts forever, and that suffering will inevitably follow "behind."

HS 127

大有好笑事，
略陳三五箇。
張公富奢華，
孟子貧轗軻。
只取侏儒飽，
不憐方朔饑。
巴歌唱者多，
白雪無人和。

HS 128

老翁娶少婦，
髮白婦不耐。
老婆嫁少夫，
面黃夫不愛。
老翁娶老婆，
一一無棄背。
少婦嫁少夫，
兩兩相憐態。

HS 127

There are many amusing things;
Let me tell you a few in brief.
Lord Zhang flourished in wealth and luxury,
4 While Master Meng suffered in his poverty.[1]
They only made sure that the dwarfs were fed,
Indifferent to the hunger of Dongfang Shuo.[2]
Many people will sing the Song of Ba,
8 While few harmonize with the White Snow tune.[3]

HS 128

If an old man takes a young wife,
His wife won't stand his white hair.
If an old lady marries a young man,
4 The man won't love her sallow looks.
If an old man takes an old lady,
Neither will abandon the other.
If a young wife marries a young man,
8 The two of them will love each other.

---

1 Lord Zhang is probably Zhang Yi 張儀, a talented Warring-States era debater, who was criticized by Mencius (Master Meng).

2 Dongfang Shuo was a talented scholar, but also a sort of court entertainer to Emperor Wu of the Han. He complained that Emperor Wu fed his jester-dwarfs well, while he left talented scholars to starve.

3 This alludes to an anecdote from an essay attributed to Song Yu 宋玉 (3rd cent. BCE), in which he considers the best music as that which is appreciated by only a few connoisseurs.

HS 129

雍容美少年，
博覽諸經史。
盡號曰先生，
皆稱為學士。
未能得官職，
不解秉耒耜。
冬披破布衫，
蓋是書誤己。

HS 130

鳥語情不堪，
其時臥草庵。
櫻桃紅爍爍，
楊柳正毿毿。
旭日銜青嶂，
晴雲洗淥潭。
誰知出塵俗，
馭上寒山南。

HS 129

Gentle and polite, that lovely youth;
He's broadly examined the classics and histories.
All refer to him as "Master,"
Everyone calls him "scholar."
But he never could get an official post,
And he doesn't know how to wield a plow.
In winter he wears a tattered hempen shirt;
It seems that his books have deceived him.

HS 130

When I can't stand the feelings the birdsongs evoke,
I lie down within my thatched hut.
Then cherry and peach blossoms gleam in their crimson,
And the willow branches fly about in tangles.
The setting sun is swallowed by the green cliffs,
And reflections of clouds are washed in the clear pond.
Who knows how to escape this vulgar dust
And drive his carriage up the south side of Cold Mountain?

HS 131

昨日何悠悠，
場中可憐許。
上為桃李徑，
下作蘭蓀渚。
復有綺羅人，
舍中翠毛羽。
相逢欲相喚，
脈脈不能語。

HS 132

丈夫莫守困，
無錢須經紀。
養得一牸牛，
生得五犢子。
犢子又生兒，
積數無窮已。
寄語陶朱公，
富與君相似。

HS 131

Yesterday—how serene it was!
And lovely it was in the clearing.
Above, paths through the peach and plum trees,
Below, an islet amid the thoroughwort and calamus.
And there in the lodge was a girl in patterned silk,
Adorned with kingfisher plumes in her hair.
I met her and wanted to call out to her,
But only gazed on her and could not speak.

HS 132

A real man should not bear his poverty;
If he has no cash, he must make his plans.
Let him look after a single cow,
So it can give birth to five calves.
If the calves then give birth in turn,
There will be no end to what he accrues.
Send word then to Master Tao Zhu:
"I'm as wealthy as you are!"[1]

1 Tao Zhu was the name taken by the famous strategist Fan Li 范蠡 after he left his position as an advisor to the king of Yue. In one early text he advises a man to invest in cattle as a reliable road to wealth.

HS 133

之子何惶惶，
卜居須自審。
南方瘴癘多，
北地風霜甚。
荒陬不可居，
毒川難可飲。
魂兮歸去來，
食我家園葚。

HS 134

昨夜夢還家，
見婦機中織。
駐梭如有思，
擎梭似無力。
呼之迴面視，
況復不相識。
應是別多年，
鬢毛非舊色。

HS 133

That guy is really frantic—
For he has to be careful in making his home.
In the south, miasmal plagues are great,
And in the north, the wind and frost are bad.
He can't reside in a backwoods corner,
Nor drink from a poisoned stream.
Oh soul! Come back home again,
And eat the mulberries from my garden![1]

HS 134

Last night I returned home in a dream,
And saw my wife weaving at her loom.
She stopped the shuttle as if she brooded on something,
Held up the shuttle as if too weak to go on.
I called to her, and she turned to look—
But it seemed like she didn't know me.
It must be I've been gone for so many years,
And the hair at my temples is not the color it was.

---

1 This last couplet alludes to "The Summons to the Soul," a poem from the *Chuci*, in which the speaker attempts to recall a soul to its recently deceased body. Here, the soul stands in for the restless subject of the poem, who is discontentedly seeking the best place to live.

HS 135

人生不滿百，
常懷千載憂。
自身病始可，
又為子孫愁。
下視禾根下，
上看桑樹頭。
秤鎚落東海，
到底始知休。

HS 136

世有一等流，
悠悠似木頭。
出語無知解，
云我百不憂。
問道道不會，
問佛佛不求。
子細推尋著，
茫然一場愁。

HS 135

A human life won't last a hundred years,
Yet it's filled with a thousand of worry.
Just as soon as you're over your own illness,
You stew over your sons and grandsons.
Below, you check the earth where the sprouts take root;[1]
Above, you look at the mulberry trees.
If you drop a steelyard weight in the eastern sea,
You know it's over when it hits bottom.[2]

HS 136

There's a certain type in the world,
Unconcerned and wooden-headed.
When he opens his mouth, no wisdom;
He says, "Nothing ever worries me!"
Ask him about the Way—he doesn't understand;
Ask him about the Buddha—he hasn't sought him.
If you carefully look into this matter:
It's all muddled, a realm of grief.

1 Reading variant *tu* 土 ("earth") for *xia* 下 ("below").

2 A proverbial expression that refers to finality—when something heavy falls into the water, it does not stop until it hits bottom. "Hit bottom" can also mean "in the end"—here referring that human toil only ends with death.

HS 137

董郎年少時，
出入帝京裏。
衫作嫩鵝黃，
容儀畫相似。
常騎踏雪馬，
拂拂紅塵起。
觀者滿路傍，
箇是誰家子。

HS 138

箇是誰家子，
為人大被憎。
癡心常憒憒，
肉眼醉瞢瞢。
見佛不禮佛，
逢僧不施僧。
唯知打大臠，
除此百無能。

HS 137

When Master Dong was just a young man,[1]
He frequented the Imperial City,
With his shirt fashioned of goose-yellow silk,
And features worthy of a painting.
Always he rode a snow-stepping steed,[2]
Stirring clouds of red dust wherever he went.
And gawkers filled the road to watch:
"Just who is that guy anyway?"

HS 138

Just who is that guy anyway?
His character hated by everyone.
A foolish mind, always excitable,
And carnal sight blind in drunkenness.
He sees Buddha but won't pay him courtesy,
He sees a monk but won't give him charity.
He only knows how to bolt down his meat,
And he's useless for everything else.

1 This is Dong Xian 董賢, a sexual favorite of the doomed last ruler of the Eastern Han dynasty, Aidi 哀帝 (r. 7–1 BCE). He was treated with excessive favor due to his handsome looks, until a palace coup forced him to commit suicide after the death of his master.
2 "Snow-stepping steed" was a steed with four white hooves.

HS 139

人以身為本，
本以心為柄。
本在心莫邪，
心邪喪本命。
未能免此殃，
何言懶照鏡。
不念金剛經，
却令菩薩病。

HS 140

城北仲家翁，
渠家多酒肉。
仲家婦死時，
吊客滿堂屋。
仲翁自身亡，
能無一人哭。
喫他盃臠者，
何太冷心腹。

HS 139

People should take their Selves as their root,
And this root has its application in the mind.
Don't let that root in the mind go bad;
For if the mind goes bad, you lose your life's root.
People can never avoid this misfortune!
Why say you're too lazy to look in the mirror?
If you don't chant the Diamond Sutra,
It makes the bodhisattvas sick.

HS 140

Old Man Zhong from north of town:
His house has so much meat and wine.
So when the lady of the Zhong family died,
The mourners filled his halls and rooms.
But when Old Man Zhong himself passed away,
Not a single person wept.
Those who drank his wine and ate his meat—
How cold-hearted they were!

HS 141

下愚讀我詩，
不解却嗤誚。
中庸讀我詩，
思量云甚要。
上賢讀我詩，
把著滿面笑。
楊脩見幼婦，
一覽便知妙。

HS 142

自有慳惜人，
我非慳惜輩。
衣單為舞穿，
酒盡緣歌啐。
當取一腹飽，
莫令兩脚儽。
蓬蒿鑽髑髏，
此日君應悔。

HS 141

When a fool reads my verse,
He doesn't understand, but scoffs at it anyway.
When a middling type reads my verse,
He ponders, then says, "That's important!"
When a wise one reads my verse,
His whole face breaks out in a smile.
When Yang Xiu saw "young bride,"
With one glance, he knew it was "marvelous."[1]

HS 142

Naturally there are stingy people in the world,
But I am not the stingy type.
My clothes are thin, they wear out as I dance;
All the wine is gone, because my song urged the drinking.
One ought to eat until you're full, though,
So that you're legs don't tire out.
When brambles grow through your skull:
You'll regret it on that day.[2]

1 An anecdote from the *Shishuo xin yu* describes how Yang Xiu, an advisor to the warlord Cao Cao 曹操, competed with his master to solve a rebus inscribed on a stele in honor of a Lady Cao. Part of the rebus involved interpreting the phrase "young bride" to mean "youthful woman" 少女—the component parts of the character *miao* 妙, or "marvelous."

2 Regret that you did not take your pleasure while alive.

HS 143

我行經古墳，
淚盡嗟存沒。
塚破壓黃腸，
棺穿露白骨。
攲斜有瓮缾，
振撥無簪笏。
風至攪其中，
灰塵亂坲坲。

HS 144

夕陽赫西山，
草木光曄曄。
復有朦朧處，
松蘿相連接。
此中多伏虎，
見我奮迅鬣。
手中無寸刃，
争不懼懾懾。

HS 143

In my travels I passed ancient mounds;
My tears ran out as I lamented life and death.
The tombs had collapsed, weighing down on the yellow wood;[1]
And the coffins were pierced, exposing white bones within.
All askew, the urns and the vases;
I barged about, found no hairpins or tallies.[2]
A wind came up, stirring everything up;
Ashes and dust flew everywhere.

HS 144

The evening sun shines on the western hills;
Plants and trees give off a sparkling light.
But there are also places of gloom therein,
Where pines and vines all intertwine.
And there are many tigers crouching there;
When they see me, they rage and bristle.
I've not the smallest blade at hand,
So shouldn't I tremble in fright?

---

1 Literally, "yellow innards," the cypress wood from which coffins were made.

2 Members of the official class would have been buried with these ornaments as a sign of the offices they held while alive. The poet is gesturing to the futility of such demonstrations when one is dead.

HS 145

出身既擾擾，
世事非一狀。
未能捨流俗，
所以相追訪。
昨吊徐五死，
今送劉三葬。
終日不得閑，
為此心悽愴。

HS 146

有樂且須樂，
時哉不可失。
雖云一百年，
豈滿三萬日。
寄世是須臾，
論錢莫啾唧。
孝經末後章，
委曲陳情畢。

HS 145

Since I've been in this world, it's a muddle—
And there are so many different jobs to do.
I could never abandon everyday things,
And so I still bustle off to manage them.
Yesterday I mourned the death of Xu Five;
Today, I take Liu Three to his grave.
All day long, not a moment of rest;
Because of this, I'm always tormented.

HS 146

When you have music, take your joy for now;
You mustn't lose this chance!
Though people speak of "a hundred years,"
We don't even last thirty thousand days.
Our time in this world is but a moment,
So don't bicker over the cost of things!
The last chapter of the *Classic of Filial Piety*
With some subtlety tells of this matter.[1]

1 The reference to the *Classic of Filial Piety* is satiric. The final chapter of this work describes the proper demeanor for someone mourning the death of a parent; one phrase says, "He is not happy when he hears music."

HS 147

獨坐常忽忽，
情懷何悠悠。
山腰雲縵縵，
谷口風颼颼。
猿來樹嫋嫋，
鳥入林啾啾。
時催鬢颯颯，
歲盡老惆惆。

HS 148

一人好頭肚，
六藝盡皆通。
南見驅歸北，
西逢趂向東。
長漂如汎萍，
不息似飛蓬。
問是何等色，
姓貧名曰窮。

HS 147

I sit alone, ever lost in thought,
While my feelings within drift away.
Clouds trail and turn on the mountainside,
And the wind whistles at the mouth of the valley.
Gibbons come—the trees sway back and forth;
Birds enter in—the forest echoes their song.
Time hastens my gray hairs: they wither.
The year ends: I am old and grieving.

HS 148

Here's a fine figure of a man,
Conversant with all the Six Arts.
When you see him in the south, he's hurrying home north;
When you meet him in the west, he's rushing to the east.
Ever drifting like floating duckweed;
Never at rest, like drifting brambles.
If you ask him just what type he is:
His name is "Impoverished Desperation."

HS 149

他賢君即受，
不賢君莫與。
君賢他見容，
4 不賢他亦拒。
嘉善矜不能，
仁徒方得所。
勸逐子張言，
8 拋却卜商語。

HS 150

俗薄真成薄，
人心箇不同。
殷翁笑柳老，
4 柳老笑殷翁。
何故兩相笑，
俱行諂誑中。
裝車競嵽嵲，
8 翻載各瀧涷。

HS 149

"If others are worthy, then you accept them;
If they're not worthy, you shouldn't be with them."
"If *you* are worthy, *they* will accept *you*;
4 And if *you're* not worthy, they'll reject you.
Praise talent, and comfort inability;
Only then will the benevolent find their place."
I urge you to follow Zizhang's words,
8 And reject the speech of Bu Shang.[1]

HS 150

The shallowness of laypeople is truly shallow;
Every human mind is different.
Grandpa Yin laughs at Gaffer Liu,
4 And Gaffer Liu laughs at Grandpa Yin.
And why should they laugh at teach other,
Since *both* are adept at craftiness?
Vie in loading your carts high as a mountain:
8 They'll tip over, and all you'll have is a mess.

1 The whole poem adapts *Analects* 19.3. In it, the advice of Confucius' disciple Bu Shang is contrasted unfavorably with the more compassionate and self-critical views of another disciple, Zizhang.

HS 151

是我有錢日，
恆為汝貸將。
汝今既飽暖，
見我不分張。
須憶汝欲得，
似我今承望。
有無更代事，
勸汝熟思量。

HS 152

人生一百年，
佛說十二部。
慈悲如野鹿，
瞋忿似家狗。
家狗趂不去，
野鹿常好走。
欲伏獮猴心，
須聽師子吼。

HS 151

In the days when I had money,
I would always lend some to you.
Now that you are already well-fed and warm,
When you see me you won't share.
You should remember that when you were in want,
That's like me now hoping for something.
Having and not having will come in their turn—
I urge you to think long on that.

HS 152

Human life, a hundred years;
The Buddha's words in twelve sections.[1]
Compassion is like a wild deer,
While wrath is like the household dog.
Drive away the dog, but he always comes back,
While the deer is always eager to flee.
If you wish to subdue your monkey-mind,
Then you must heed the lion's roar.[2]

---

1 A reference to a traditional way of organizing scriptures in the Buddhist tradition; the categories include types of preaching—*gāthas*, *avadānas*, conventional sermons, etc.

2 A common metaphor for the Buddha's preaching.

HS 153

教汝數般事，
思量知我賢。
極貧忍賣屋，
纔富須買田。
空腹不得走，
枕頭須莫眠。
此言期衆見，
挂在日東邊。

HS 154

寒山多幽奇，
登者皆恒懾。
月照水澄澄，
風吹草獵獵。
凋梅雪作花，
杌木雲充葉。
觸雨轉鮮靈，
非晴不可涉。

HS 153

Let me teach you a few things—
If you think about it, you'll know I'm wise.
If you're very poor, refrain from selling the house;
When wealthy again, you must buy fields.
Don't run on an empty stomach,
Don't sleep with a comfortable pillow.[1]
These words I hope everyone will see—
Let them be hung high with the rising sun.

HS 154

There are many hidden marvels at Cold Mountain;
Climbers there are constantly in awe.
Moon shines on the water, clear and still;
Wind blows, rustling through the grass.
Snow puts flowers on withered plum branches,
And clouds serve as leaves for branchless trees.
Things are even more fresh and lively when it rains,
But you can only get there when it's clear.

1 I.e., do not make yourself at ease when you go to sleep, or you will lose alertness.

HS 155

有樹先林生，
計年逾一倍。
根遭陵谷變，
葉被風霜改。
咸笑外凋零，
不憐內紋綵。
皮膚脫落盡，
唯有貞實在。

HS 156

寒山有躶蟲，
身白而頭黑。
手把兩卷書，
一道將一德。
住不安釜竈，
行不齎衣裓。
常持智慧劍，
擬破煩惱賊。

HS 155

There's a tree that predates the forest;
More than twice as old, if you count up the years.
Its roots have met the change of valley and slope,[1]
And its leaves have been altered by wind and frost.
Everyone laughs at its withered exterior,
No one cherishes its fine patterns within;
And when its bark is stripped away,
Only then will its pure essence remain.

HS 156

There's a naked beast on Cold Mountain,
With a white body and black hair.
In his hand he holds a two-chapter book,
One called "Way," the other "Power."[2]
At home he has not set up his pan and stove,
And when he goes out he wears no cassock.
He always grasps a sword of wisdom,
Planning to smash the *kleśa* bandits.

1 A recurring Chinese image describes the immense passage of time as the period it takes for a valley to become a hill, and vice versa.
2 The *Laozi* (which is also called *The Classic of the Way and Its Power*).

HS 157

有人畏白首，
不肯舍朱紱。
采藥空求仙，
根苗亂挑掘。
數年無效驗，
癡意瞋怫鬱。
獵師披袈裟，
元非汝使物。

HS 158

昔時可可貧，
今朝最貧凍。
作事不諧和，
觸途成倥傯。
行泥屢腳屈，
坐社頻腹痛。
失却斑猫兒，
老鼠圍飯瓮。

HS 157

There are people who fear their white hair,
Yet they're unwilling to resign their vermilion sash.[1]
They pick herbs, vainly seeking Transcendence,
Wildly digging up roots and sprouts.
For several years now they've had no success,
Their foolish thoughts turn angry and uneasy.
They're hunters who don the cassocks of monks—
They shouldn't use those from the start.

HS 158

I was rather poor in past days,
But this morning I'm most poor and cold!
Nothing I do works out the way it should,
And everything turns to grief and hardship.
When walking through mud I always slip;
When I attend the season festivals I get indigestion.
And now when I've lost my tortoiseshell cat,
The rats are circling the rice jar.

1 A sign of official office.

HS 159a

我見世間人，
堂堂好儀相。
不報父母恩，
方寸底模樣。
欠負他人錢，
蹄穿始惆悵。
箇箇惜妻兒，
爺孃不供養。
兄弟似冤家，
心中長悵怏。
憶昔少年時，
求神願成長。
今為不孝子，
世間多此樣。
買肉自家噇，
抹觜道我暢。
自逞說嘍囉，
聰明無益當。
牛頭努目瞋，
出去始時鄉。

HS 159a[1]

I see the people in this world:
Loftily they put on a distinguished air.
But they don't repay their parents' grace;
Just what is their inch of heart like?
When they owe others money,
They'll only grieve when their hoofs are worn away.[2]
Each only cherishes wife and child,
And does not provide for Mom and Dad.
Brothers treat each other as enemies,
Their minds ever moody and annoyed.
I remember when they were still young,
Their parents prayed that they'd grow up well.
And now they've become unfilial sons—
Most people in the world are like this.
They buy meat and eat it for themselves,
Wipe their beaks and say "I feel great!"
They boast of themselves and their witty speech,
Their unsurpassable cleverness.
But when the bull-headed demons glare at them in rage,[3]
Only then will they want to escape.

1 I am certain that 159 consists of two poems, for the following reasons: 1) ll 21–36 have no thematic connection to ll. 1–20; 2) ending a poem with a threat of Hell (ll. 19–20) is common elsewhere in the corpus (see HS 56, SD 5, SD 12); 3) ll. 21–22 rhyme—a frequent technique employed in the opening couplet of a Hanshan poem.

2 This refers to a popular Buddhist belief that those who die owing money will be reborn as a beast of burden that will repay the debt with its labor.

3 Bull-headed demons serve as guards in Hell.

HS 159b

擇佛燒好香，
揀僧歸供養。
羅漢門前乞，
趂却閒和尚。
不悟無為人，
從來無相狀。
封疏請名僧，
䞋錢兩三樣。
雲光好法師，
安角在頭上。
汝無平等心，
聖賢俱不降。
凡聖皆混然，
勸君休取相。
我法妙難思，
天龍盡迴向。

HS 159b

They select a Buddha, burn fine incense,
Pick a monk, do him homage, make offerings.
But as for the Arhat begging before their gates—
They drive him away as an idle cleric.[1]
They are not aware that the man without activity
Never displays exterior signs.[2]
They compose letters to invite eminent monks,
Offering money two or three times.
Yunguang was a fine dharma master,
But now he wears horns on his head.[3]
If you don't have a mind that holds all things as equal,
Then sages and worthies will not descend to you.[4]
The common and the sagely are intermingled;
I urge you to cease making distinctions.
My dharma is marvelous, hard to think about;
But all magic beings will pledge their deeds to it.

---

1 This poem draws on legends concerning Piṇḍola (Bintoulu 賓頭盧), one of the Arhats who the Buddha requested should remain behind in samsara to aid practitioners. He was famous for his gluttony (in reality, "greedy" for the charity of pious laypeople), and as a result he became in East Asia a sort of patron of monastery refectories. He is said to wander the world in disguise, visiting monasteries and maigre feasts prepared by lay believers. An early tale describes how he was driven away by a servant from a maigre feast because he was dressed in rags.

2 "Without activity" (*wu wei*) generally has Daoist associations; but in Buddhism it can describe the conduct of enlightened beings, who do not generate karma in whatever they do.

3 Yunguang was an antinomian monk he boasted that he was above the monastic precepts. He was reborn as a cow.

4 The typically Confucian terms "sages and worthies" here probably stand in for Buddhas and bodhisattvas.

HS 160

我今稽首禮，
無上法中王。
慈悲大喜捨，
名稱滿十方。
衆生作依怙，
智慧身金剛。
頂禮無所著，
我師大法王。

HS 161

可貴天然物，
獨一無伴侶。
覓他不可見，
出入無門戶。
促之在方寸，
延之一切處。
你若不信受，
相逢不相遇。

HS 160

I now bow low in reverence
To the unsurpassed Prince of the Dharma.
Compassionate, delighted in surrendering all;
Praise of his name fills the ten directions.
All living things depend on him;
All-wise, with a body of diamond.
I prostrate myself before the one without attachments;
I take the Great Dharma Prince as my teacher.

HS 161

Precious, this natural thing!
Alone it stands, without a match.
Look for it—it's invisible,
Goes in and out, no gate or door.
Contract it all within the inch of mind,
Or stretch it out to everywhere.
But if you don't have faith in it,
You'll meet it and not notice it.

HS 162

余家有一窟，
窟中無一物。
淨潔空堂堂，
光華明日日。
蔬食養微軀，
布裘遮幻質。
任你千聖現，
我有天真佛。

HS 163

男兒大丈夫，
作事莫莽鹵。
勁挺鐵石心，
直取菩提路。
邪路不用行，
行之枉辛苦。
不要求佛果，
識取心王主。

HS 162

There is a cavern at my house,
And in that cavern—not a single thing.
It is clean and pure, empty and lofty,
And light shines in it, bright as the sun.
Plain fare nourishes my trivial form,
And a hempen robe covers my illusory substance.
You can have the manifestation of a thousand sages;
I have the truly existing Buddha.

HS 163

Gentlemen, you stalwart fellows,
Don't be careless in what you do.
Firmly hold on to your mind of iron and stone,
Follow directly the path to enlightenment.
Useless to go down heterodox paths;
If you do, you'll just bring yourself pointless hardship.
Don't *seek out* the fruits of Buddhahood;
Rather, recognize the Prince and Master of your mind.

HS 164

粵自居寒山，
曾經幾萬載。
任運遯林泉，
棲遲觀自在。
寒巖人不到，
白雲常靉靆。
細草作臥褥，
青天為被蓋。
快活枕石頭，
天地任變改。

HS 165

可重是寒山，
白雲常自閑。
猿啼暢道內，
虎嘯出人間。
獨步石可履，
孤吟藤好攀。
松風清颯颯，
鳥語聲喧喧。

HS 164

Since I've been living at Cold Mountain,
Thousands and thousands of years have passed.
I surrender to fate, hide in forests and streams;
Whether at rest or wandering I observe the spontaneous.
People don't come to Cold Cliff,
And the white clouds are lowering around me.
Slender grass serves as my mattress,
And the blue sky is my canopy overhead.
Delighted, I pillow my head on a stone,
As Heaven and Earth surrender to change.

HS 165

Cold Mountain, something to be valued;
White clouds always drifting calmly.
Gibbons chatter, singing a song of the Way;[1]
Tigers roar as they come out among men.
I can navigate the rocks in my solitary walk,
Climbing the vines as I chant poems alone.
The clear pine-wind whistles and roars,
And the speech of birds twitters around me.

---

1 Line three is open to interpretation and revision. I agree with Xiang Chu and assume that the line is textually corrupted and should read 猿啼唱道曲. This is based on a similar line in Shide SD 54, and on a number of Chan texts that speak of people "singing a song of the Way" (*chang dao qu* 唱道曲). This might also clarify the fourth line, in which the tigers "roar"; the verb used here is also the noise produced by a form of Daoist hygienic breath control. In that case, both gibbons and tigers are civilized religious cultivators, and both the poet and nature are making appropriate noises (this sound production continues in lines 6–8).

HS 166

閑自訪高僧，
煙山萬萬層。
師親指歸路，
月挂一輪燈。

HS 167

閒遊華頂上，
日朗晝光輝。
四顧晴空裏，
白雲同鶴飛。

HS 168

世有多事人，
廣學諸知見。
不識本真性，
4 與道轉懸遠。
若能明實相，
豈用陳虛願。
一念了自心，
8 開佛之知見。

HS 166

In leisure I visit a lofty monk,
Through myriad on myriad of misty hills.
The master himself points the road back home:
Where the moon hangs its single-wheeled lamp.

HS 167

At leisure I wander on Huading Peak;[1]
Sunlight reveals all in its daytime glow.
I look all around me within this clear void;
The white clouds are flying with the cranes.

HS 168

In the world there are men of many affairs,
Broad in learning, with many fields of knowledge.
But they don't recognize their original true nature,
4 And drift further and further apart from the Way.
If you can illumine your actual attributes,[2]
There is no point in making empty vows.
With one thought you comprehend the Self-Mind,
8 And you reveal the Buddha's "field of knowledge"!

1 Huading is the highest peak of the Tiantai range.

2 "Attributes" here (*xiang*) is meant to translate *lakṣaṇa*, a term broadly meant to refer to defining characteristics. Often enlightened beings are said to transcend them or to not manifest them (as in l. 6 of 159b, "exterior signs"). However, here *shi xiang* is meant to indicate "true" identity or attributes, independent of the attributes manifested in samsara.

HS 169

寒山有一宅，
宅中無闌隔。
六門左右通，
堂中見天碧。
房房虛索索，
東壁打西壁。
其中一物無，
免被人來惜。
寒到燒軟火，
飢來煮菜喫。
不學田舍翁，
廣置牛莊宅。
盡作地獄業，
一入何曾極。
好好善思量，
思量知軌則。

HS 169

On Cold Mountain there's a dwelling;
And the dwelling has no fence or bars.
Its six gates are open to left and right,
The blue sky can be seen from the hall.
Room after room—all are empty,
The east walls knock into the west walls.
I don't keep anything inside
So people won't come and gawk at it.
When it's cold I'll light a modest fire,
When hungry I'll boil some greens to eat.
I'm not like those old geezer farmers,
Who keep lots of oxen on their ranch.
All of them build up Hell-bound karma.
When will it end once they enter there?
Think about this now good and hard,
Then you'll see the principle behind it.

HS 170

儂家暫下山，
入到城隍裏。
逢見一群女，
端正容貌美。
頭戴蜀樣花，
燕脂塗粉膩。
金釧鏤銀朵，
羅衣緋紅紫。
朱顏類神仙，
香帶氛氳氣。
時人皆顧眄，
癡愛染心意。
謂言世無雙，
魂影隨他去。
狗齩枯骨頭，
虛自舐脣齒。
不解返思量，
與畜何曾異。
今成白髮婆，
老陋若精魅。
無始由狗心，
不超解脫地。

HS 170

For a time I descended from the mountain,
Coming at last to the city moat.
And there I met a flock of girls,
Poised they were, with lovely features.
Shu-blossom ornaments on their heads,[1]
Rouge on cheeks, their painted powder sleek.
Gold bracelets filigreed with silver blooms,
Silken robes, all red, crimson, and purple.
Ruddy faces, like those of a goddess,
Fragrant sashes in a billowing haze.
Men nowadays all give them the eye,
With foolish lust that would stain their minds.
They think those girls have no peer in the world,
And their soul-shadows chase after them.
Now if a dog chews on a dried-up bone,
In vain he licks his chops and teeth.
They don't know how to ponder this truth:
That they're no different from the beasts.
Now girls all turn to white-haired grannies,
Old and mean, like mountain ghouls.
If you act with a dog's mind from the start,
You won't reach the place of liberation.

1 The region of Shu (modern Sichuan) was famous in Tang times for the artificial flower-ornaments it produced.

HS 171

一自遯寒山，
養命餐山果。
平生何所憂，
此世隨緣過。
日月如逝川，
光陰石中火。
任你天地移，
我暢巖中坐。

HS 172

我見世間人，
茫茫走路塵。
不知此中事，
將何為去津。
榮華能幾日，
眷屬片時親。
縱有千斤金，
不如林下貧。

HS 171

Since I've hidden away at Cold Mountain,
I've been eating mountain fruit, nourishing my life.
What do I have to worry about in this existence?
I pass through this world following my karma.
Days and months pass like a departing stream,
Time is just a flash from a flint stone.
You may change along with Heaven and Earth;
But I'll delight in sitting here on my cliff.

HS 172

I see the people of this world:
At a loss, they hurry through the dust on the road.
They don't know the Central Matter,[1]
So how can they make a future path?
How many days can glory last?
Dear ones are close to you but a short time.
Even if you had a thousand pounds of gold,
It's better to live impoverished in the woods.

1 The Buddhist Dharma—here, the phrase is synonymous with 箇中意 in HS 105.

HS 173

自聞梁朝日，
四依諸賢士。
寶志萬迴師，
四仙傅大士。
顯揚一代教，
任持如來使。
造建僧伽藍，
信心歸佛理。
雖乃得如斯，
有為多患累。
與道殊懸遠，
折東補西爾。
不達無為功，
損多益少利。
有聲而無形，
至今何處去。

HS 173

I myself have heard of the days of the Liang,
The Four Steadfasts, all worthy gentlemen;[1]
Baozhi, teacher Wanhui,[2]
The Four Transcendents, Great Layman Fu.[3]
They made manifest the Faith for an entire age;
They took up the task as the Tathāgata's emissaries,
Establishing and constructing monasteries.
Their minds of faith submitted to the Buddha's laws.
But even though they accomplished such things,
Actions of merit bring many worrisome burdens.
They drifted further apart from the Way,
Merely took from the east to fill in for the west.[4]
They didn't comprehend the merit of non-action,
The benefit of losing much and gaining little.[5]
Though they made their names, they themselves have vanished,
And where have they all gone now?

1 Commentators are not agreed on the meaning of *si yi* here, which could either mean "four groups that may be relied on" or "four kinds of reliance."

2 Baozhi (418–514) was a famous wonder-working monk. Wanhui was an early Tang monk; the poem seems to have confused his era here.

3 The text's si xian 四仙 (Four Transcendents) is a puzzle. Usually "transcendents" is a Daoist term, so it is unclear whether the poet is conflating Daoist and Buddhist teachings here (not impossible in the Tang era), or whether this is an error for something else. Various lists of Daoist adepts have been suggested. Xiang Chu makes a reasonable if unprovable speculation that the text has miscopied Sizhou 泗州, another name for the eminent Liang-era mong Sengqie 僧伽. I have chosen to leave the text as is. Great Layman Fu (497–569) became a prominent teacher and propagator of the faith during the Liang era.

4 A proverb meaning that one makes no forward gains, but merely distributes what is already there for appearance's sake.

5 Or, "so their loss was great, with increasingly little profit." How one reads the line depends on whether the poet is emphasizing the seeming paradox of non-action.

HS 174

吁嗟貧復病，
為人絕友親。
甕裏長無飯，
甑中屢生塵。
蓬庵不免雨，
漏榻劣容身。
莫怪今憔悴，
多愁定損人。

HS 175

養女畏太多，
已生須訓誘。
捺頭遣小心，
鞭背令緘口。
未解秉機杼，
那堪事箕箒。
張婆語驢駒，
汝大不如母。

HS 174

Alas! To be poor and sick as well,
And cut off from contact with friend or kin.
A storage jar often empty of rice
And a steamer that tends to collect dust.
An overgrown hut that doesn't keep out the rain,
A broken-down couch with no room for one.
Don't wonder that I've grown haggard now:
Too many worries will wear you down.

HS 175

We fear having too many daughters;
But once one is born, we must train her carefully.
Force her head down and compel her to be careful,
Beat her on the back to make her shut her mouth.
If she never understands how to use loom and shuttle,
How can she serve with dustpan and broom?[1]
As Granny Zhang said to her donkey's foals,
"You're not as big as your mother!"[2]

1 "Serve with dustpan and broom" is a standard locution for getting married.
2 I.e., every generation is worse than the one before it.

HS 176

秉志不可卷，
須知我匪席。
浪造山林中，
獨臥盤陀石。
辯士來勸余，
速令受金璧。
鑿牆植蓬蒿，
若此非有益。

HS 177

以我棲遲處，
幽深難可論。
無風蘿自動，
不霧竹長昏。
澗水緣誰咽，
山雲忽自屯。
午時庵內坐，
始覺日頭暾。

HS 176

I hold to my will, it cannot be rolled up;
You must understand—I am not a mat.[1]
Freely I go off to the mountain wood,
Where I lie alone on a great flat rock.
Expert debaters come to persuade me,
To make me accept gold and jade right away.[2]
If you bore through the wall to plant brambles,
There's no benefit to be found in that!

HS 177

This place in which I rest and wander:
Hard to describe how secluded and deep.
Vines rustle on their own when there's no wind,
And bamboo thickets are dark, even when there's no fog.
For whom does this stream water gurgle?
The mountain clouds will swiftly pile up.
I stay seated in my hut until noon,
Only then aware of the sunlight's growing warmth.

---

1 An allusion to from the *Shijing*, #26 (*Bo zhou*): "My mind is not a mat, / it cannot be rolled up."

2 Gifts from the ruler who wishes to lure him from his reclusion and to give him official office.

HS 178

憶昔遇逢處，
人間逐勝遊。
樂山登萬仞，
愛水泛千舟。
送客琵琶谷，
攜琴鸚鵡洲。
焉知松樹下，
抱膝冷颼颼。

HS 179

報汝修道者，
進求虛勞神。
人有精靈物，
無字復無文。
呼時歷歷應，
隱處不居存。
叮嚀善保護，
勿令有點痕。

HS 178

I recall all my past encounters,
When I'd go on splendid travels in the world of men.
I delighted in hills—climbed up ten thousand fathoms;
I loved the waters—floated in a thousand boats.
I saw off my guests at Lute Valley,[1]
Walked with zither under my arm on Parrot Island.[2]
How could I have known, here under this pine tree,
I'd sit hugging my knees, chilled by the gale?

HS 179

I tell all of you who practice the Way:
Vain to labor your spirit in striving.
People have a pure essence within,
Without a name, without a sign.
Call it and it clearly answers,
Yet has no hidden place to dwell.
Be careful to guard it always—
Don't let it have a spot or scratch.

---

1 Lute Valley is still unidentified. It may simply be an invention for the purposes of parallelism.
2 A scenic islet in the Yangtze near Wuhan, frequently visited by travelers.

HS 180

去年春鳥鳴，
此時思弟兄。
今年秋菊爛，
此時思發生。
淥水千場咽，
黃雲四面平。
哀哉百年內，
腸斷憶咸京。

HS 181

多少天台人，
不識寒山子。
莫知真意度，
喚作閑言語。

HS 182

一住寒山萬事休，
更無雜念挂心頭。
閑書石壁題詩句，
任運還同不繫舟。

HS 180

Last year, when the spring birds sang—
That's when I longed for my brothers.
This year, when the fall chrysanthemums bloomed—
That's when I longed for burgeoning spring.
Clear waters gurgle in a thousand places,
And brown clouds fill the entire sky.
Alas—within this life of mine
I think with broken heart of Xianyang.[1]

HS 181

So many people at Tiantai
Do not recognize Master Cold Mountain.
No one knows his true meaning,
Calling it merely idle speech.

HS 182

As soon as I moved to Cold Mountain, all the affairs of the world ceased,
And no more were there distracting thoughts to hang upon the mind.
Idly I write on stony cliffs, inscribing my lines of verse;
Turning myself over to fate just like an unmoored boat.[2]

---

1 This poem is one of the most enigmatic in the collection. Some commentators point to the "brown clouds" in line six, which occurs in Tang poetry as an image of warfare on the frontiers; combining this with the final reference to Xianyang, they interpret it as the poet's lament over the fall of the capital area during the An Lushan 安祿山 rebellion in 756, reading the longing for spring in line four as a longing for the flourishing days of the Tang. However, granted the general lack of historical specificity in the collection overall, this is still highly speculative.

2 This and HS 271 are the only two poems that refer to the poet writing poems on natural surfaces.

HS 183

可惜百年屋，
左倒右復傾。
牆壁分散盡，
木植亂差橫。
甎瓦片片落，
朽爛不堪停。
狂風吹驀塌，
再豎卒難成。

HS 184

精神殊爽爽，
形貌極堂堂。
能射穿七札，
讀書覽五行。
經眠虎頭枕，
昔坐象牙牀。
若無阿堵物，
不啻冷如霜。

HS 183

What a pity, this hundred-year old house;[1]
The left side collapsed, the right side aslant.
The walls have all melted away,
And the wooden supports stick out across.
Roof tiles have fallen off one by one;
No one can halt its rotting away.
If a gust of wind were to blow, it would collapse at once;
Then it would be impossible to build it up again.

HS 184

Your spirit may be very clear and quick,
Your body quite tall and imposing.
You can shoot arrows through seven layers of armor,
Or read books five lines at a time.
You may have slept on a tiger-head pillow,
Or always sat on an ivory couch.
But if you didn't have "that thing,"[2]
You'd only be as desolate as frost.

1 The term "hundred years" here informs the reader that the house is an allegory for human life.

2 *E du wu* ("that thing") is a euphemism for money; first mentioned in an anecdote from the *Shishuo xinyu*, in which the aristocrat Wang Yifu used the term because he would not pollute his mouth with the word for money.

HS 185

笑我田舍兒，
頭頰底縶澀。
巾子未曾高，
腰帶長時急。
非是不及時，
無錢趂不及。
一日有錢財，
浮圖頂上立。

HS 186

買肉血㶑㶑，
買魚跳鱍鱍。
君身招罪累，
妻子成快活。
纔死渠便嫁，
他人誰敢遏。
一朝如破牀，
兩箇當頭脫。

HS 185

They laugh at me since I'm a hick:
My looks are pretty crude,
And my head cloth is never tall enough,
And I always pull my belt too tight.
It's not that I'm not caught up with the times—
I'm just too broke to follow them.
When one day I've got the money,
I'll wear a *pagoda* on my head.

HS 186

Buy meat with the blood still trickling,
Buy fish while they still leap about.
You are summoning the burden of sin on yourself,
Just to make wife and children happy.
When you finally die she'll marry again,
And no one else dare prevent it.
One day, you two will be like a broken bed,
Pulled apart from head to foot.[1]

1 Though the last image may simply refer to the separation of husband from wife, it is not impossible that it may refer to the punishments both wife and husband will receive in Hell—since Hell punishments are mentioned almost inevitably in the HS and SD poems as the result of meat-eating. Compare HS 36, 95, 159a, 233; and SD 2, 4, 5, 12, and 39.

HS 187

客難寒山子，
君詩無道理。
吾觀乎古人，
貧賤不為恥。
應之笑此言，
談何疏闊矣。
願君似今日，
錢是急事爾。

HS 188

從生不往來，
至死無仁義。
言既有枝葉，
心懷便險詖。
若其開小道，
緣此生大偽。
詐說造雲梯，
削之成棘刺。

HS 187

A guest criticized Master Cold Mountain:
"Your poems make no sense."
"But I've observed the Ancients:
With them, poverty and humble station were not shameful."
He replied to this: "I laugh at your words!
How wide of the mark your conversation is!
I wish you would act as the moderns do:
Money is the important thing."

HS 188

From birth, no traveling about;
Until death, no "kindness" or "justice."[1]
Once your words shoot off branches and leaves,
Then the heart harbors deviousness.
If you open access to the petty ways,
Then they will give rise to great fraud.
Falsely persuade someone to build a scaling ladder,
Then whittle it away until it turns to splinters.

1 Both of these lines have their roots in sentiments expressed in early Daoist texts: people who are content do not travel about; and the truly contented country has no need for the Confucian virtues of kindness (*ren*) or justice (*yi*).

HS 189

一缾鑄金成，
一缾埏泥出。
二缾任君看，
那箇缾牢實。
欲知缾有二，
須知業非一。
將此驗生因，
修行在今日。

HS 190

摧殘荒草廬，
其中煙火蔚。
借問群小兒，
生來凡幾日。
門外有三車，
迎之不肯出。
飽食腹膨脝，
箇是癡頑物。

HS 189

One vessel is cast from gold,
Another is produced from clay.
I give you both to look at now:
Which one is more authentic?
If you wish to know that there are two different vessels,
You must know that their originary acts differed.[1]
Use this to investigate the Cause of our birth;
Practice is something you should cultivate now.

HS 190

Shattered is the lodge in the field of weeds;
Within, the smoke and fire have spread.
I ask all the small children within:
"Just how long has it been since you were born?
There are three carts outside the gate
To welcome you, but you won't come out!
You're eating until your bellies swell:
What a bunch of fools you are!"[2]

1 "Originary acts" is my translation for *ye*, the Buddhist term for actions that have karmic consequences. The poet is suggesting that the reason that people differ is because of their different karmic inheritances, just as vessels are made of different material.

2 This poem (as well as HS 255) is based on the famous "burning house" parable in the Lotus Sutra.

HS 191

有身與無身，
是我復非我。
如此審思量，
遷延倚巖坐。
足間青草生，
頂上紅塵墮。
已見俗中人，
靈牀施酒果。

HS 192

昨見河邊樹，
摧殘不可論。
二三餘幹在，
千萬斧刀痕。
霜凋萎疏葉，
波衝枯朽根。
生處當如此，
何用怨乾坤。

HS 191

"There is a body and there is not a body;
There is a Self and there is not a Self."
I deeply pondered in this way,
Lingering as I sat, leaning against a cliff.
Green grass grew between my feet,
And red dust settled on top of my head.
You can already see people from the customary world
Offering wine and fruit at my spirit altar.[1]

HS 192

Yesterday I saw a tree by the river,
All shattered beyond description.
Two or three of its trunks remained,
With a million scars of axe and blade.
Frost had blighted its sparse and drooping leaves,
While currents pummeled its withered roots.
Our sphere of life is just like that;
Pointless to resent Heaven and Earth.

1 The speaker has remained so motionless in mediation the local populace assumes either he is dead or that he is the statue of a divinity.

HS 193

余見僧繇性希奇，
巧妙間生梁朝時。
道子飄然為殊特，
二公善繪手毫揮。
逞畫圖真意氣異，
龍行鬼走神巍巍。
饒邈虛空寫塵跡，
無因畫得志公師。

HS 194

久住寒山凡幾秋，
獨吟歌曲絕無憂。
蓬扉不掩常幽寂，
泉涌甘漿長自流。
石室地鑪砂鼎沸，
松黃柏茗乳香甌。
飢餐一粒伽陀藥，
心地調和倚石頭。

HS 193

I've seen Sengyou, by nature rare and strange;[1]
Clever and marvelous, he lived his days in the time of the Liang court.
Daozi was light and free, truly exceptional;[2]
These two masters were good at painting, their hands wielded well the brush.
Flaunting their art, sketching the true, the force of their thoughts was distinctive:
Dragons moved forth and ghosts rushed out, their gods were awe-inspiring.
Granted they could draw illusions and sketch their dusty traces;
Yet they had no skill in capturing Master Baozhi.[3]

HS 194

Long I've lived at Cold Mountain—for several autumns now.
I hum a song to myself; I've got absolutely no worries.
I do not shut my rustic door, yet it's always secluded and still;
The stream bubbles up with sweet nectar, always flowing on its own.
In stone chambers, in earthen furnace my smelting cauldron seethes;
Pine Yellow and cypress brew, and pots of fragrant tea.
When hungry I eat a single grain of the agada drug;
I adjust the ground of my mind as I lean against a stone.[4]

---

1 Zhang Sengyou (fl. 490–540), a famous painter of religious subjects in the sixth century.

2 Wu Daozi (b. 680), one of the most famous painters of the Tang era.

3 For Baozhi, see HS 173. A Chan legend describes how the emperor once commanded Zhang Sengyou to paint Baozhi. Baozhi then slashed his own face with his finger, revealing a twelve-faced Guanyin. Sengyou could not complete his task.

4 There are a number of references to drugs and potions here usually associated with Daoist practices. "Pine Yellow" refers to a brew made from pine tree pollen. Both that and tea made from cypress leaves were said to have positive medicinal effects. "Fragrant tea" here is literally "milk fragrance," a term used to refer to the fragrance from freshly brewed tea that comes from the cloudy froth on top of the infusion; in the Tang era, tea was still largely valued for its medicinal properties and was not a common beverage. "Agada" is a medicine mentioned in sutras, also used as a metaphor for helpful remedies (including spiritual ones). Though the import of the lines evokes Daoist longevity practices, the images themselves combine alchemy with evocations of reclusion and Buddhism.

HS 195

丹丘迥聳與雲齊，
空裡五峰遙望低。
雁塔高排出青嶂，
4 禪林古殿入虹蜺。
風搖松葉赤城秀，
霧吐中巖仙路迷。
碧落千山萬仞現，
8 藤蘿相接次連谿。

HS 196

千生萬死凡幾生，
生死來去轉迷盲。
不識心中無價寶，
猶似盲驢信腳行。

HS 197

老病殘年百有餘，
面黃頭白好山居。
布裘擁質隨緣過，
4 豈羨人間巧樣模。

HS 195

Cinnabar Hill thrusts far above, level with the clouds;[1]
The Five Peaks in the middle of the sky seem low when seen from afar.[2]
Goose pagodas, loftily arrayed, emerge from the green cliffs;[3]
Old buildings in the meditation forest merge into a rainbow.[4]
Wind shakes the pine tree needles, and Redwall is magnificent;[5]
Mist comes out of Mid-Cliff, concealing the Transcendents' path.[6]
A thousand hills in the blue empyrean display their myriad-fathomed height;
And rattan vines join together in the midst of connected vales.

HS 196

A thousand lives, ten thousand deaths—how many lives in all?
Life and death shall come and go, and we grow more blind and lost.
We do not recognize the priceless jewel hidden within our minds;
And we are like a sightless ass whose legs carry him where they will.

HS 197

Old and sick, in waning years, with so many lingering attachments;
Features sallow, hair all white, I prefer to live in the hills.
A hempen robe enwraps my substance as I follow my karma;
How should I envy the human realm with all its clever types?

---

1 Cinnabar Hill was a poetic name for Tiantai common in Daoist circles.
2 The Five Peaks are five mountains in the Tiantai range near the Guoqing Temple.
3 "Goose pagoda" (*yan ta*) is an elegant term for a Buddhist monastery pagoda.
4 "Meditation wood" (*chan lin*) is an elegant term for a monastery; the assembly of practicing monks is the monastery's "forest."
5 Redwall is another prominent peak in the Tiantai range.
6 Mid-cliff Temple (*zhongyan si*) was one of the monasteries in the Tiantai complex.

心神用盡為名利，
百種貪婪進己軀。
浮生幻化如燈燼，
塚內埋身是有無。

HS 198

世間何事最堪嗟，
盡是三途造罪楂。
不學白雲巖下客，
一條寒衲是生涯。
秋到任他林落葉，
春來從你樹開花。
三界橫眠閑無事，
明月清風是我家。

HS 199

昔年曾到大海遊，
為采摩尼誓懇求。
直到龍宮深密處，
金關鎖斷主神愁。

They exhaust their mind and spirit for the sake of fame and profit;
With a hundred kinds of covetousness they advance themselves.
Their illusory floating life is like embers in a lamp;
And that body buried in the tomb—does it even exist or not?

HS 198

In this world, what affair is most worthy of our sighs?
It's entirely those sinning fools on the Three Evil Paths.
They won't imitate the man on the cliff among white clouds—
Whose single humble monastic robe is the sum of all he owns.
Autumn arrives: let the woods drop their leaves as they will;
Spring comes: let the trees blossom if they wish.
I rest where I please in the Three Realms, idle, with nothing to do.[1]
The bright moonlight and the clear breeze: these are my home.

HS 199

In years gone by, I once went traveling by the great sea;
It was to collect the *maṇi* gem for which I had sworn to search.[2]
I went straightaway to the dragon's palace in a hidden secluded place;
I broke open its golden locks—the presiding gods were worried.

1 The three realms (*jing*; *dhātu*) constitute samsara: the realm of form, the realm of desire, and the realm of formlessness. They are often used as a poetic substitution for samsara itself.

2 The *maṇi* gem is used in sutras as a metaphor for something particularly precious; often (as here) as a symbol for the Buddha Nature within everyone.

龍王守護安耳裏，
劍客星揮無處搜。
賈客却歸門內去，
8 明珠元在我心頭。

HS 200

衆星羅列夜明深，
巖點孤燈月未沈。
圓満光華不磨瑩，
挂在青天是我心。

HS 201

千年石上古人蹤，
萬丈巖前一點空。
明月照時常皎潔，
不勞尋討問西東。

HS 202

寒山頂上月輪孤，
照見晴空一物無。
可貴天然無價寶，
埋在五陰溺身軀。

The dragon king guarded the gem, placed it inside his ear;
His swordsmen flashed their blades like stars, there was no place I could look.
This merchant then went home again, and I went inside my gate;
8 The bright pearl all along was contained within my mind.

HS 200

All the stars form their ranks; the night, radiant, grows late;
A spot on the cliff—a single lamp—the moon has yet to set.
Complete and perfect radiance, beyond all polishing;
Hanging in the black night sky—*that* is my Mind.

HS 201

On rocks traversed for a thousand years, the traces of the Ancients;
Before a cliff a myriad fathoms high, a single spot of void.
When the bright moon shines, it is always radiant and clear—
No need to take the trouble and ask which way to go.

HS 202

On the heights of Cold Mountain the moon's disc hangs alone;
It illuminates the clear void; not a single thing exists.
The precious, heaven-innate invaluable jewel
Is buried in the five skandhas, drowned within the Self.[1]

1 The skandhas ("bundles") are the five psycho-physical constituents that construct the false consciousness of a Self.

HS 203

我向前谿照碧流，
或向巖邊坐磐石。
心似孤雲無所依，
悠悠世事何須覓。

HS 204

我家本住在寒山，
石巖棲息離煩緣。
泯時萬象無痕跡，
舒處周流遍大千。
光影騰輝照心地，
無有一法當現前。
方知摩尼一顆珠，
解用無方處處圓。

HS 205

世人何事可吁嗟，
苦樂交煎勿底涯。
生死往來多少劫，
東西南北是誰家。

HS 203

Sometimes I go to the stream and see my reflection in its deep-blue current;
Sometimes I go to the side of the cliff and sit on a slab of stone.
My mind is like a solitary cloud that relies on nothing;
Indifferent to the affairs of this world—for what else should I seek?

HS 204

My original home is here at Cold Mountain;
I perch at rest on stony cliffs, away from troublesome ties.
When they are swept away, the myriad phenomena leave no trace behind;
Then when they manifest, they flow everywhere, covering a billion worlds.
Light and shadow go rushing forth, reflected on the mind;
Yet not a single dharma manifests itself before me.[1]
Now I know of the *maṇi* gem, that one single pearl:
There is not one method in using it; it is perfect in every way.[2]

HS 205

What matter among the people of the world is worthy of lament?
Bitterness and joy will burn together and never have an end.
Birth and death, coming and going, for so many kalpas;
East and West and South and North—for whom is this a home?

---

1 This is the meaning of "dharma" (*fa*) as an individual phenomenon within samsara.

2 For the *maṇi* gem, see HS 199. There are two significant puns here. *Wufang* ("no method," "no predetermined method") can also mean "not square." *Yuan* can mean "round" but also "perfect."

張王李趙權時姓，
六道三途事似麻。
只為主人不了絕，
遂招遷謝逐迷邪。

HS 206

余家本住在天台，
雲路煙深絕客來。
千仞巖巒深可遯，
萬重谿澗石樓臺。
樺巾木屐沿流步，
布裘藜杖繞山迴。
自覺浮生幻化事，
逍遙快樂實善哉。

HS 207

憐底眾生病，
餐嘗略不猒。
蒸豚搵蒜醬，
炙鴨點椒鹽。

Zhang and Wang and Li and Zhao—merely provisional names;[1]
In the Six Courses and Three Evil Paths, events are as hemp in the field.[2]
This is all because the one in charge does not know how to end it:
He summons cycles of change and fading, pursuing delusion and perversity.

HS 206

My original home is here in the Tiantai Mountains;
Mist is thick on the road through the clouds, preventing wanderers from coming.
Cliffs and hills a thousand fathoms high are dense, providing refuge;
And a myriad bends of the ravine stream contain stone halls and terraces.
With head cloth of birch bark and wooden clogs I stroll, following the current;
With hempen robe and goosefoot staff I circle about the hills.
I've become aware of the illusory things of this floating life;
And the pleasures of free and easy wandering are truly wonderful!

HS 207

A pity, this sickness in sentient beings:
In eating, nearly insatiate.
Steamed piglet soaked in garlic sauce,
Roast duck with salted peppers,

1 These are four of the most common surnames. The poem is saying that our name in any incarnation is merely a provisional and impermanent identity.

2 "As hemp in a field" is a common metaphor to describe something as beyond counting.

去骨鮮魚膾，
兼皮熟肉臉。
不知他命苦，
只取自家甜。

HS 208

讀書豈免死，
讀書豈免貧。
何以好識字，
識字勝他人。
丈夫不識字，
無處可安身。
黃連搵蒜醬，
忘計是苦辛。

HS 209

我見瞞人漢，
如籃盛水走。
一氣將歸家，
籃裏何曾有。

Fresh minced fish, their bones removed,
Broth of meat simmered with its skin.[1]
They don't know the suffering of other living things,
Only choose the sweetness for themselves.

HS 208

Reading books won't help you escape death;
Reading books won't help you escape poverty.
So why should you want to be literate?
Being literate makes you better than others.
If a full-grown man is illiterate,
There is no place where he can find rest.
Like goldthread soaked in garlic sauce,
His disordered plans are bitter indeed![2]

HS 209

I've seen the guys who cheat others—
They're like people running with a basketful of water.
In all one rush they hurry home,
To find there's nothing left in their basket.

---

1 The precise contents of these dishes are somewhat open to debate. I take the suggestion that *lian* in line 6 ("face") can also be read as "meat broth."

2 For goldthread, famous for its bitterness, see also HS 76. Garlic sauce as well would have a pungent, bitter quality. Most commentators are agreed that the text's *wang ji* 忘計 ("forget plans") is a corruption of the text here. I follow the suggestion that *wang ji* 妄計 ("wild plans") is the likely reading. The meaning would then suggest that the disordered thinking of an illiterate man would bring bitterness to his life equivalent to the taste of goldthread in garlic sauce.

我見被人瞞，
一似園中韭。
日日被刀傷，
天生還自有。

HS 210

不見朝垂露，
日爍自消除。
人身亦如此，
閻浮是寄居。
切莫因循過，
且令三毒袪。
菩提即煩惱，
盡令無有餘。

HS 211

水清澄澄瑩，
徹底自然見。
心中無一事，
水清眾獸現。

And I see people who have been cheated—
They're exactly like leeks in the garden.
Every day they're cut with a knife,
But still preserve their heaven-endowed life.

HS 210

Haven't you seen the dripping dew at dawn?
It glitters in the sun, then vanishes away.
The Selves of humans are also like this;
Jambudvīpa is but a temporary lodge.[1]
You must not pass your life casually,
But eliminate the Three Poisons.[2]
Bodhi and *kleśa* are the same—[3]
Make sure that there are no remainders.[4]

HS 211

When water is clear, lucid, and lustrous,
You can see right down to the bottom.
If there is not a single matter in your mind,
It's like when all the beasts appear in clear water.[5]

1 In traditional Buddhist cosmology, Jambudvīpa is the world continent on which we ourselves live.

2 For the Three Poisons, see HS 91.

3 For *kleśa*, see HS 156. This is a classic Mahayana rejection of dualism; enlightenment itself is potentially an obstruction if one becomes preoccupied with it and continues to think in a dualistic manner as a goal to be obtained.

4 That is, lingering karmic attachments and effects that could interfere with enlightenment.

5 Wen Jiao 溫嶠 (3rd cent.) once had to cross a body of water reputed to have evil spirits. He lit a rhinoceros horn as a torch and was able to illuminate the creatures hidden in the water.

心若不妄起，
永劫無改變。
若能如是知，
是知無背面。

HS 212

自從到此天台境，
經今早度幾冬春。
山水不移人自老，
見却多少後生人。

HS 213

說食終不飽，
說衣不免寒。
飽喫須是飯，
著衣方免寒。
不解審思量，
只道求佛難。
迴心即是佛，
莫向外頭看。

If you do not let your mind rise wildly,
There will be no change for countless kalpas.
And if you are able to understand this way,
8 This understanding has no front or back.

HS 212

From when I arrived in this Tiantai realm
Until now, I've already lived several winters and springs.
The landscape never changes, but people do grow old;
And now I see quite a few people younger than me.

HS 213

You'll never be full just talking of food;
And talking of clothes won't keep off the cold.
To eat your fill, you must have food;
4 And putting on clothes will keep off the cold.
But you don't know how to ponder this;
You just say it's hard to search for the Buddha.
Return to the mind—*that* is the Buddha;
8 Do not look for him without.

HS 214

可畏輪迴苦，
往復似翻塵。
蟻巡環未息，
六道亂紛紛。
改頭換面孔，
不離舊時人。
速了黑暗獄，
無令心性昏。

HS 215

可畏三界輪，
念念未曾息。
纔始似出頭，
又卻遭沈溺。
假使非非想，
蓋緣多福力。
争似識真源，
一得即永得。

HS 214

How frightful the suffering of the karmic wheel!
Back and forth we go, like roiling dust.
We're ants that never rest in their circling tour,
While the Six Courses teem with our riot.
Change your head or alter your face—
You can't get away from who you were.
Be quick to understand the gloom of Hell;
Do not let your mind and nature darken.

HS 215

How frightful the wheel of the Three Realms!
Thought after thought, we never rest.
Just when it seems that you've managed to escape,
Once again you sink down deep and drown.
Even if you make it to "No Non-Thoughts,"[1]
(No doubt because of your good karma),
How is that like recognizing the *true* source?
Once found, it's kept forever.

1 This is the fourth Heaven in the Realm of Formlessness, and the highest Heaven in which one can be reborn while still remaining within the three realms of samsara. This is a considerable achievement, but still nothing compared to obtaining enlightenment through the realization of one's true nature.

HS 216

昨日遊峰頂，
下窺千尺崖。
臨危一株樹，
風擺兩枝開。
雨漂即零落，
日曬作塵埃。
嗟見此茂秀，
今為一聚灰。

HS 217

自古多少聖，
叮嚀教自信。
人根性不等，
高下有利鈍。
真佛不肯認，
置功枉受困。
不知清淨心，
便是法王印。

HS 216

Yesterday I went roaming atop the peaks,
Peering down a thousand-foot bluff.
Over the edge, a single tree—
The wind had blasted its limbs apart.
The rain had scoured it bare;
The sun had baked it into dust.
I sighed to see such flourishing
Now reduced to a pile of ash.

HS 217

From ancient times, so many sages
Have earnestly taught faith in oneself.
The essential nature of each person differs,
Lofty or low, it is sharp or dull.
Yet they won't acknowledge the true Buddha;
They focus on earning merit and uselessly suffer.
They don't realize that a pure and clean mind
Is precisely the seal of the Dharma Prince.

HS 218

我聞天台山，
山中有琪樹。
永言欲攀之，
莫曉石橋路。
緣此生悲歎，
索居將已暮。
今日觀鏡中，
颯颯鬢垂素。

HS 219

養子不經師，
不及都亭鼠。
何曾見好人，
豈聞長者語。
為染在薰蕕，
應須擇朋侶。
五月販鮮魚，
莫教人笑汝。

HS 218

I have heard about the Tiantai Mountains:
That in those mountains there is a snow-gem tree.
For long I have wished to climb it,
But no one knew the road to Stone Bridge.
Because of this I utter a grieving sigh:
Living as a hermit—soon dusk will fall.
Today when I looked in the mirror,
My grizzled locks let droop their gray.

HS 219

If you raise a son without a teacher,
He won't come up to a city station rat.[1]
When would he ever meet good people,
And how hear the words of his elders?
Because either basil or bluebeard will stain him,[2]
You must select his companions.
If you try to sell fish in the Fifth Month,
Make sure not to become a laughingstock![3]

1 A proverb holds that "city station rats know much"—that is, their urban experience makes them cleverer than other rats.

2 That is, the son will inevitably take on the "odor" of his friends. The bluebeard plant has blossoms that emit a stench when crushed, as opposed to the sweetness of basil.

3 Fish markets in summer would have a particularly strong odor; as with line five, the implication is that association with those who lack virtue will damage one's own virtue and/or reputation.

HS 220

徒閉蓬門坐，
頻經石火遷。
唯聞人作鬼，
不見鶴成仙。
念此那堪說，
隨緣須自憐。
迴瞻郊郭外，
古墓犁為田。

HS 221

時人見寒山，
各謂是風顛。
貌不起人目，
身唯布裘纏。
我語他不會，
他語我不言。
為報往來者，
可來向寒山。

HS 220

In vain I close my weed-covered gate and sit;
I watch time pass: sparks struck from a stone.
I have only heard of people turning to ghosts;
Have yet to see cranes turn into Transcendents.
Thinking on this, how can I bear to speak of it?
I'll follow my fate and look after myself.
Just turn and look to the city outskirts,
Where old tomb mounds are ploughed into fields.

HS 221

When people of this age see me, Hanshan,
Each says that I'm a madman.
My features do not arouse attention,
And my body is wrapped only in a hempen robe.
What *I* say they don't understand,
And what *they* say I wouldn't speak.
That's why I reply to passers-by:
"You should come to Cold Mountain!"

HS 222

自在白雲閑，
從來非買山。
下危須策杖，
4 上險捉藤攀。
澗底松長翠，
谿邊石自斑。
友朋雖阻絕，
8 春至鳥喧喧。

HS 223

我在村中住，
眾推無比方。
昨日到城下，
4 却被狗形相。
或嫌褲太窄，
或說衫少長。
攣却鷂子眼，
8 雀兒舞堂堂。

HS 222

Freely the white clouds move at their leisure;
This has never been a bought mountain.[1]
Below, it is treacherous—I must rely on a staff;
Above, it is steep—I ascend by clinging to vines.
In the bottom of ravines, the pines are ever turquoise,
And by the side of the stream the rocks are spotted.
Though I am cut off from all companions,
When spring comes, the birds are set singing.

HS 223

When I lived in the village,
Everyone claimed I had no equal.
But yesterday I went to the city,
And even the dogs were sizing me up.
Some judged that my trousers were too narrow,
And some said that my shirt was a little long.
Once you've closed the eyes of the kestrel,
The sparrows will dance in their pride.

1 The Buddhist philosopher Zhi Dun 支遁 (314–366) once sought to buy a mountain on which he could practice reclusion. He dropped the attempt when he was greeted with derision.

HS 224

生死元有命，
富貴本由天。
此是古人語，
吾今非謬傳。
聰明好短命，
癡騃却長年。
鈍物豐財寶，
醒醒漢無錢。

HS 225

國以人為本，
猶如樹因地。
地厚樹扶疏，
地薄樹憔悴。
不得露其根，
枝枯子先墜。
決陂以取魚，
是取一期利。

HS 224

"Life and death have their determined times;
Wealth and status come from Heaven."
These are the words of the Ancients;
I'm not passing on anything absurd.
The clever usually have short lifespans,
While the foolish are long-lived.
The dull are rich with wealth and treasure,
While clear-minded men have no money.

HS 225

The state takes its people as its root,
Just as a tree relies on the soil.
If the soil is deep, then the tree grows thick;
If the soil is shallow, then the tree withers.
Make sure its roots are not exposed;
Then branches dry out and the fruit falls early.
If you breach the dike to catch fish,
Then you're just taking the profit of a moment.[1]

1 This poem likely is meant to emphasize that the well-being of the people is essential for a healthy state. The last image describes someone who has broken the dike around a fishpond and drained away the water in order to make it easier to catch fish; in the process, he kills all the fish and ruins the pond.

HS 226

眾生不可說，
何意許顛邪。
面上兩惡鳥，
心中三毒蛇。
是渠作障礙，
使你事煩拏。
舉手高彈指，
南無佛陀耶。

HS 227

自樂平生道，
煙蘿石洞間。
野情多放曠，
長伴白雲閑。
有路不通世，
無心孰可攀。
石床孤夜坐，
圓月上寒山。

HS 226

You can't explain sentient beings:
So unexpectedly crazy and twisted.
In their faces, two evil birds;
In their minds, three poisonous snakes.[1]
These things serve as obstructions
And force you to serve disorder.
Raise your hand high and snap your fingers—[2]
All hail the Lord Buddha!

HS 227

I delight in the path of my common life,
Mid misty vines and stony grottoes.
I often indulge my taste for the country,
And I've long befriended the idle white clouds.
There's a road here but it doesn't reach the world;
My mind void, to what could I cling?
On a stony bench I sit in the lone night,
While a round moon ascends on Cold Mountain.

1 The three poisonous snakes are the same as the Three Poisons (see HS 91). The two evil birds are open to interpretation. Xiang Chu sees it as shrikes and owls; though he notes traditions that mention two birds as symbolic of ignorance on the one hand and perception and thought on the other. There is also an Indian parable about a two-headed bird—one head only eats sweet fruit; the other head, jealous, eats poison until they both die.

2 For the significance of snapping one's fingers in Buddhist texts, see HS 34.

HS 228

大海水無邊，
魚龍萬萬千。
遞互相食噉，
兀兀癡肉團。
為心不了絕，
妄想起如煙。
性月澄澄朗，
廓爾照無邊。

HS 229

自見天台頂，
孤高出眾群。
風搖松竹韻，
月現海潮頻。
下望山青際，
談玄有白雲。
野情便山水，
本志慕道倫。

HS 228

The waters of the great sea are endless—
Million upon million of fish and dragons,
All of them devouring each other,
Dim-witted, foolish lumps of flesh.
Because their minds do not know how to cease,
Disordered thoughts rise up like smoke.
But if the moon of their natures shines clear and bright,
Then all would open up, illumined endlessly.

HS 229

I've seen for myself the heights of Tiantai,
Lone and lofty, rising above the other hills.
Winds harmonize as they shake pine and bamboo,
Sea tides go in and out when the moon appears.
Below, I gaze to the edge of mountain's green,
And I discuss mysteries with the white clouds.
My taste for the countryside fits with this landscape;
And my aspirations admire these companions of the Way.[1]

1 Probably referring to the monks of Tiantai.

HS 230

三五癡後生，
作事不真實。
未讀十卷書，
強把雌黃筆。
將他儒行篇，
喚作賊盜律。
脫體似蟫蟲，
齩破他書帙。

HS 231

心高如山嶽，
人我不伏人。
解講圍陀典，
能談三教文。
心中無慚愧，
破戒違律文。
自言上人法，
稱為第一人。
愚者皆讚歎，
智者撫掌笑。
陽餤虛空花，
豈得免生老。

HS 230

There are a few fools, younger than me,
Who are not honest in their actions.
Before reading even ten chapters of anything,
4 They go wild with their orpiment brush.[1]
They label writings about Confucian conduct
As the rules for dealing with bandits and thieves.
They elude me just like the silverfish
8 Who gnaw away at the book wraps.

HS 231

His mind is as lofty as the mountains;
He's adamant when arguing with others;
He knows how to lecture on Vedic texts,
4 He can discuss the scriptures of the Three Teachings.[2]
In his mind, no sense of shame;
He violates precepts, goes against the vinaya.
He himself speaks a "superior man's Dharma,"[3]
8 And he's acclaimed as the best of all.
The foolish all praise him and sigh,
While the wise clap their hands and laugh.
He's but a flickering flame, spots in the eye—[4]
12 How can he avoid rebirth and growing old?

---

1 Orpiment (*cihuang*) was a sulfur compound used to wipe out textual errors (like modern correction fluid). This refers to ill-educated people who have the temerity to "correct" writings by others.

2 Confucianism, Buddhism, and Daoism.

3 "Superior man's dharma" (*shang ren fa*) is mentioned in Buddhist texts as the sin of claiming superior wisdom or knowledge without justification.

4 "Spots in the eye" is literally "empty flowers" (*xu kong hua*), and is used for spots or floaters that occur in one's vision.

不如百不解，
靜坐絕憂惱。

HS 232

如許多寶貝，
海中乘壞舸。
前頭失却桅，
4 後頭又無柁。
宛轉任風吹，
高低隨浪簸。
如何得到岸，
8 努力莫端坐。

HS 233

我見凡愚人，
多畜資財穀。
飲酒食生命，
4 謂言我富足。
莫知地獄深，
唯求上天福。
罪業如毗富，
8 豈得免灾毒。

It would be better to understand nothing,
And sit tranquilly, severing all worries.

HS 232

So great a number of treasures
Are carried in a broken-down barge on the sea.
It has lost its mast in front,
And there is no rudder behind.
It tosses and turns, blown with the wind;
It rises and falls, rocked by the waves.
How will it ever reach the shore?
Strive diligently—don't just sit![1]

HS 233

I see the ordinary fools:
They store away so much wealth and grain.
They drink wine, eat living beings,
And think that they are rich enough.
None of them know the depths of Hell;
They only seek the blessings of the highest heaven.[2]
Yet their sinful karma is like Mount Vipula;[3]
How can they avoid this disastrous peril?

---

1 The poem may be taken as an allegory of the individual human (barge), endowed with the Buddha nature (treasures), attempting to reach enlightenment (the shore). The poem urges striving and activity, and not merely quiet sitting in meditation.

2 That is, they imagine their own virtue will allow them to be reborn in the highest of the Buddhist heavens.

3 Name given to a number of mountains in India noted for their size.

財主忽然死，
爭共當頭哭。
供僧讀文疏，
空是鬼神祿。
福田一箇無，
虛設一群禿。
不如早覺悟，
莫作黑暗獄。
狂風不動樹，
心真無罪福。
寄語兀兀人，
叮嚀再三讀。

HS 234

勸你三界子，
莫作勿道理。
理短被他欺，
理長不奈你。
世間濁濫人，
恰似鼠粘子。
不見無事人，
獨脫無能比。

If a man of wealth suddenly dies,
All vie at once in gathering to mourn him.
They feast the monks who conduct the service;
But the service is merely a gift to ghosts.
Nothing accrues to his Field of Blessings;[1]
It's useless to assemble this flock of baldies.
It's better to awaken from the start—
Don't do things that lead to the Hell of ignorance.
Be a tree unmoved by gusts of wind,
With a true mind beyond sin or merit.
I send word to all you dim-witted ones:
Read this carefully, over and over!

HS 234

I urge you, dwellers in the Three Realms:
Don't behave irrationally!
If you're short in reason, then you'll be abused;
If you're long in it, they won't put up with you.
All the vulgar, polluted people of the world
Are exactly like rats with burrs in their fur.[2]
Don't you see the man without affairs,[3]
Who stands alone, with no one who can rival him?

---

1 A Field of Blessings (*fu tian*) is the positive karma an individual accrues through charitable actions, especially gifts to monks. The point here is that the services may allow the deceased to gain some karmic benefit; but he has already lost the opportunity to make any significant gains in his karma while alive.

2 I.e., they cannot free themselves from passion and anger.

3 That is, a being who no longer produces karmically significant actions.

早須返本源，
三界任緣起。
清淨入如流，
莫飲無明水。

HS 235

三界人蠢蠢，
六道人茫茫。
貪財愛婬欲，
心惡若豺狼。
地獄如箭射，
極苦若為當。
兀兀過朝夕，
都不別賢良。
好惡總不識，
猶如豬及羊。
共語如木石，
嫉妒似顛狂。
不自見己過，
如豬在圈臥。
不知自償債，
却笑牛牽磨。

Return to the original source right away;
In the Three Realms, you're subject to dependent origination.[1]
Enter the pure and clear stream of Thusness;
Do not drink the water of ignorance.

HS 235

People in the Three Realms writhe and wriggle;
People on the Six Courses are vast in their throngs.[2]
Greedy for wealth, lustful in their desires,
Their minds wicked like wild dogs and wolves.
Thrown into hell like a speeding arrow—
How to withstand such extreme suffering?
Muddle-headed they pass each day,
Unable to distinguish what is worthy.
They can't recognize the good and the wicked,
They're as stupid as pigs or sheep.
Talking to them is like speaking to wood or stone;
And they're demented in their jealousies.
They cannot observe their own faults,
Like pigs reclining in their sty;
They don't understand the debts they owe,
And laugh instead at the ox dragging a millstone.[3]

1 "Dependent origination" (*pratītya-samutpāda*; *yuanqi*): the twelve-stage chain of causality that leads from ignorance to samsaric rebirth.

2 For Six Courses, see HS 72 and note.

3 For the significance of this image, see HS 159a and note.

HS 236

人生在塵蒙，
恰似盆中蟲。
終日行遶遶，
不離其盆中。
神仙不可得，
煩惱計無窮。
歲月如流水，
須臾作老翁。

HS 237

寒山出此語，
復似顛狂漢。
有事對面說，
所以足人怨。
心真出語直，
直心無背面。
臨死度柰河，
誰是嘍囉漢。
冥冥泉臺路，
被業相拘絆。

HS 236

Human life in this dust-covered world
Is just like a bug in a bowl.
All day it travels round and round,
But it never gets out of the bowl.
Transcendence cannot be attained;
Kleśa strategems are endless.
The months and years flow on like water,
And suddenly you're an old man.

HS 237

I, Hanshan utter these words
As if I were some madman.
When I have something, I say it face-to-face,
So it's enough to cause resentment.
But since my mind is true, my words are direct,
And my direct mind has no front or back:
When you've died and you're crossing the Hopeless River,[1]
Then who is the clever talker?
Gloomy the road to the Underworld;
You're bound by your karmic misdeeds.

1 For the Hopeless River, see HS 74.

HS 238

我見多知漢，
終日用心神。
岐路逞嘍囉，
4 欺謾一切人。
唯作地獄滓，
不修正直因。
忽然無常至，
8 定知亂紛紛。

HS 239

寄語諸仁者，
復以何為懷。
達道見自性，
4 自性即如來。
天真元具足，
修證轉差迴。
棄本却逐末，
8 只守一場獃。

HS 238

I've seen those know-it-alls
Who employ mind and spirit all day long,
Showing off their clever words at the crossroads,
Cheating everyone they meet.
They only become the dregs of Hell,
Don't cultivate upright karma.
When Impermanence comes upon them,
Certainly things will be thrown into chaos.

HS 239

I send word to all you benevolent types,
What are you all concerned about?
Penetrate the Way, see your Self-Nature,
The Self-Nature that is the Tathāgata.
Your natural purity is already complete;
Cultivation and realization would force you further awry.
If you abandon the root to pursue the branches,
Really, that's completely stupid!

HS 240

世有一般人，
不惡又不善。
不識主人公，
隨客處處轉。
因循過時光，
渾是癡肉臠。
雖有一靈臺，
如同客作漢。

HS 241

常聞釋迦佛，
先受然燈記。
然燈與釋迦，
只論前後智。
前後體非殊，
異中無有異。
一佛一切佛，
心是如來地。

HS 240

There's a certain kind of person in the world,
Not evil, but not good either.
He doesn't recognize who his true landlord is,
But follows the tenants at every turn.
He casually wastes his time,
Completely a stupid lump of meat.
Even though he has a spirit dwelling within,
He works as if he were a tenant.[1]

HS 241

I've often heard that Śakyamuni
At first received Dīpaṃkara's recognition.[2]
Dīpaṃkara and Śakyamuni:
You can only discuss who was wise first, and who second.
But "first" and "second" are not different in essence:
In their difference there is no difference.
One Buddha, or all the Buddhas:
Their mind is the ground for the Tathāgata.

1 There may be a pun here—he possesses a spirit (literally, "spirit terrace"), so he is actually a proprietor/landlord, and not merely a tenant farmer.

2 *Shou ji* (Skt: vyākarṇa) is a Buddha's prediction to one of disciples that he too will become a Buddha in a later life. Dīpaṃkara predicted to one of his own disciples that he would become our historical Buddha (Śākyamuni).

HS 242

常聞國大臣，
朱紫簪纓祿。
富貴百千般，
貪榮不知辱。
奴馬滿宅舍，
金銀盈帑屋。
癡福暫時扶，
埋頭作地獄。
忽死萬事休，
男女當頭哭。
不知有禍殃，
前路何疾速。
家破冷颼颼，
食無一粒粟。
凍餓苦悽悽，
良由不覺觸。

HS 243

上人心猛利，
一聞便知妙。
中流心清淨，
審思云甚要。

HS 242

I've often heard of great ministers of state,
In crimson and purple, with hatpins and hat strings bestowed.[1]
They are wealthy and noble in a million different ways,
Yet they are shameless in their greed for glory.
Slaves and horses fill their residence,
Gold and silver pile up in their warehouse.
But temporary is the good karma inherited by fools;
And they're blindly set on committing Hell-bound deeds.
When they die, all their business is at an end;
Their sons and daughters arrive to mourn.
They're unaware of the calamity they'll have;
How swiftly their future passes!
Bankrupt, freezing in the wind,
With not a single grain to eat.
Frozen and starving, they bitterly lament:
All because no one woke up.[2]

HS 243

The most superior have minds acute and fierce;
Once they hear something marvelous, they know it at once.
The middling types have minds clear and pure;
After they ponder it, they say, "Quite essential!"

---

1 In the Tang bureaucracy, official status was often marked by the color of hatpins and hat strings.

2 The second half of this poem is unclear. I read it as the bad karma of the wealthy ministers inevitably affecting the status of their offspring after they die. In this case, the last half of the poem describes the suffering of their offspring, all because they (the deceased ministers) did not wake up to the evils of their behavior in time.

下士鈍暗癡，
頑皮最難裂。
直得血淋頭，
始知自摧滅。
看取開眼賊，
鬧市集人決。
死屍棄如塵，
此時向誰說。
男兒大丈夫，
一刀兩段截。
人面禽獸心，
造作何時歇。

HS 244

我有六兄弟，
就中一箇惡。
打伊又不得，
罵伊又不著。
處處無柰何，
耽財好淫殺。
見好埋頭愛，
貪心過羅剎。

The lowest of all are blunt and benighted;
It's hardest to crack their stupid hides.
Only when their heads are soaked in blood
Do they know they're doomed to destruction.
Just see the unrepentant robber—[1]
In the bustling market people come to see him die.
His corpse is thrown away like dirt—
To whom can you speak at such a time?
"Stalwart fellows," "great men":
With one chop they are cloven in twain.
Human faces, but with a bestial mind—
When will they cease their wicked deeds?

HS 244

I have six brothers,
And one among them was wicked.
We beat him—it did no good;
We berated him—it didn't take.
Hopeless in every possible way,
Greedy for wealth, fond of wild slaughter;
When he saw what he liked, he blindly wanted it,
A covetous mind worse than any demon.

1 Literally, "robber with open eyes"—i.e., quite aware that what he does is wrong.

阿爺惡見伊，
阿孃嫌不悅。
昨被我捉得，
惡罵恣情掣。
趂向無人處，
一一向伊說。
汝今須改行，
覆車須改轍。
若也不信受，
共汝惡合殺。
汝受我調伏，
我共汝覓活。
從此盡和同，
如今過菩薩。
學業攻鑪冶，
鍊盡三山鐵。
至今靜恬恬，
衆人皆讚說。

Our dad was disgusted at the sight of him,
Our mom, displeased, took a dislike to him.
So yesterday I caught hold of him,
And cursed him and dragged him off in my fury.
I drove him off to a private spot,
And told him off item by item.
"You have to change the way you've been acting—
Just as you take a different way when your cart is upset.[1]
If you don't believe what I'm saying,
I'm afraid your wickedness will bring your demise.[2]
But if you submit to my instruction,
I'll help you find a livelihood."
From then on he was completely amenable,
And now surpasses a bodhisattva!
He's studying a trade, learning how to smelt,
And he's already refined three mountains-worth of iron.
Now he's peaceable and quite content,
And everyone sings his praises.[3]

1 That is, you realize the road is poor and you must take another way if you hope to continue traveling. SD 19 uses the same image more lucidly.

2 I read 共 ("together") as an error for 恐 ("fear"), in keeping with the similar line in SD 19.

3 The six brothers are likely the six forms of consciousness (Skt: *vijñāna*: eye, ear, mouth, nose, body, mind), and the evil brother is probably the mind—the one that can cause the most trouble.

HS 245

昔日極貧苦，
夜夜數他寶。
今日審思量，
自家須營造。
掘得一寶藏，
純是水精珠。
大有碧眼胡，
密擬買將去。
余即報渠言，
此珠無價數。

HS 246

一生慵懶作，
憎重只便輕。
他家學事業，
余持一卷經。
無心裝褾軸，
來去省人擎。
應病則說藥，
方便度眾生。
但自心無事，
何處不惺惺。

HS 245

In past days I was extremely poor;
Every night I'd tally up the treasure of others.
Today I've pondered deeply:
I must take up business for myself.
I've dug up a treasure of one jewel,
One pure crystal gem.
But there are many blue-eyed foreigners
Who secretly plan to buy it from me.
So I reply to all of them:
This gem has no price.

HS 246

All my life I've been too lazy to act;
I've hated heavy things, preferred only the light.
Others may learn their occupations;
I have only a sutra in one chapter.
I have no intentions of mounting it on a scroll:
That spares me having to carry it around.
Responding to each sickness, I prescribe medicine:
Skillful Means that save all sentient beings.
Just as long as your mind is free of affairs,
It will be brilliant about everything.

HS 247

我見出家人，
不入出家學。
欲知真出家，
心淨無繩索。
澄澄孤玄妙，
如如無倚托。
三界任縱橫，
四生不可泊。
無為無事人，
逍遙實快樂。

HS 248

昨到雲霞觀，
忽見仙尊士。
星冠月帔橫，
盡云居山水。
余問神仙術，
云道若為比。
謂言靈無上，
妙藥必神秘。
守死待鶴來，
皆道乘魚去。

HS 247

I've seen people who have "left the household":[1]
They don't engage in the proper study of it.
If you want to know the *real* "leaving the household",
The mind is pure so that it has no restraints.
Pellucid, solitary, dark and mysterious,
It is as it is, relying on nothing.
It can roam here and there through the Three Realms,
And cannot be anchored to the Four Forms of Birth.[2]
The actionless one without affairs
Is truly delighted by such free wandering!

HS 248

Yesterday I went to the Abbey of Rosy Clouds,[3]
When I suddenly met Transcendent gentlemen,
With caps of stars, and moon-white capes across their shoulders;
They said they all lived amid mountains and waters.
I asked them the art of Transcendence;
They said, "What could compare to this Way!"
They claimed nothing could be more magical,
Though their marvelous herbs must be a kept a holy secret.
They watch over their deaths, awaiting the coming of the crane,
All saying they will depart by fish.[4]

---

1 I.e., become monks (*chu jia*).

2 Birth by egg, by womb, by dampness, and by transformation—inevitable ways of continuing samsaric existence.

3 A Daoist abbey or monastery (*guan*) is meant here.

4 Daoist lore often describes practitioners achieving Transcendence riding away on cranes or on fish.

余乃返窮之，
推尋勿道理。
但看箭射空，
須臾還墜地。
饒你得仙人，
恰似守屍鬼。
心月自精明，
萬象何能比。
欲知仙丹術，
身內元神是。
莫學黃巾公，
握愚自守擬。

HS 249

余家有一宅，
其宅無正主。
地生一寸草，
水垂一滴露。
火燒六箇賊，
風吹黑雲雨。
子細尋本人，
布裹真珠爾。

But I reflect on this and get to the bottom—
I reckon that all this is senseless.
Just look at an arrow shot into the sky:
In a moment it falls back to the earth.
Granted that you become a Transcendent;
But that's just a ghost living in his own corpse!
The Moon of the Mind is essentially bright,
The myriad phenomena can't compare.
If you want to know the Cinnabar Art,
There's an original spirit inside your form.[1]
Don't imitate those "Yellow Turban" lords,[2]
Preserving their folly as you keep to their model.

HS 249

There is a dwelling at my home,
A dwelling that has no proper master.
The earth part grows one inch of grass,
The water part lets drip one drop of dew,
The fire part consumes the Six Thieves,[3]
And the wind part blows away the black storm clouds.
If you carefully search for the "original person,"
It's merely a gem wrapped in hempen cloth.[4]

---

1 These four lines contrast the Daoist search of immortality (including the refinement of cinnabar as an elixir) with the Buddhist doctrine of the "Buddha Nature" that is naturally found within oneself.

2 A reference to the popular Daoist movement known pejoratively as the "Yellow Turbans," led by a proto-Daoist magician and leader Zhang Jue 張角 at the end of the second century CE.

3 The six senses: eye, ear, mouth, nose, body, and mind.

4 This poem is an allegory of the body, which is composed of four elements: earth, water, fire, and wind. While usually these elements are perceived as impermanent stuff, here the practitioner uses them to attain knowledge of the Buddha nature within (the gem wrapped in the hempen cloth of the worthless body).

HS 250

傳語諸公子，
聽說石齊奴。
僮僕八百人，
水碓三十區。
舍下養魚鳥，
樓上吹笙竽。
伸頭臨白刃，
癡心為綠珠。

HS 251

何以長惆悵，
人生似朝菌。
那堪數十年，
親舊凋落盡。
以此思自哀，
哀情不可忍。
柰何當柰何，
託體歸山隱。

HS 250

Let me tell you a story, gentlemen:
Have you heard about Shi Qinu?
He had eight hundred serving lads,
And thirty water mills.
Below his lodge he raised fish and birds,
And in his mansion he had reed-organs played.
Yet he stretched out his neck to the gleaming blade:
His foolish heart given over to Green Pearl.[1]

HS 251

Why am I always so downhearted?
Human life is like a mushroom at dawn.
How can I bear, that in a few dozen years,
My kin and acquaintance will all wither away?
Because of this, my thoughts turn to grief,
And these grieving feelings I cannot bear.
Oh what shall I do? What shall I do?
I shall give myself over to mountain reclusion.[2]

1 Shi Chong 石崇 (249–300; polite name Qinu) was a wealthy aristocrat. He was executed by the warlord Sun Xiu on trumped-up charges because Sun wanted Shi Chong's beautiful concubine Green Pearl. Green Pearl killed herself rather than leave Shi.

2 Or, "We shall shed our forms and return to the shade of the hills [in death]." The Hanshan poems use 歸 ("to return") both in the sense of entering the grave and fleeing to the hills. The fact that he often uses 隱 to mean "reclusion" may make my main translation more likely.

HS 252

繿縷關前業，
莫訶今日身。
若言由冢墓，
箇是極癡人。
到頭君作鬼，
豈令男女貧。
皎然易解事，
作麼無精神。

HS 253

我見黃河水，
凡經幾度清。
水流如急箭，
人世若浮萍。
癡屬根本業，
無明煩惱阬。
輪迴幾許劫，
只為造迷盲。

HS 252

Your tattered clothes come from your karma;
Don't curse the body that you have now.
If you say they result from the site of your graves,[1]
Then you're really a complete idiot.
In the end, when you become a ghost,
Why would you make your children poor?
This is quite clear and easy to understand—
Why are you so unperceptive?

HS 253

I see the waters of the Yellow River:
How many times have they flowed clear?
Waters rush like a speeding arrow,
While the human world is like floating duckweed.
Fools are dependent on their original karma,
Ignorance is the snare of the *kleśas*.
The wheel of rebirth turns for countless kalpas,
While they continue to act out their blindness.

---

1 I.e., that your wealth or poverty is dependent on the geomantic position of your family's burial mounds.

HS 254

二儀既開闢，
人乃居其中。
迷汝即吐霧，
醒汝即吹風。
惜汝即富貴，
奪汝即貧窮。
碌碌群漢子，
萬事由天公。

HS 255

余勸諸稚子，
急離火宅中。
三車在門外，
載你免飄蓬。
露地四衢坐，
當天萬事空。
十方無上下，
來去任西東。
若得箇中意，
縱橫處處通。

HS 254

Ever since the Two Principles opened up,[1]
Humans have dwelt in their midst.
If they wish to confuse you, they'll emit fog;
If they wish to awaken you, they'll let blow the wind;
If they care for you, then you'll be wealthy and honored;
If they wish to despoil you, you'll be impoverished.
All you men who toil away!
All affairs come from the Lord of Heaven.[2]

HS 255

I urge all of you, children:
Depart at once from the burning house!
Three carts are outside the gate;
They'll keep you from becoming aimless drifters.
In open ground, you'll sit at the crossroads,
And face the sky, where all things are Empty.
In all directions, no up or down;
You'll come and go, moving west, then east.
If you get the Central Idea of this,
Then you can reach everywhere in all directions![3]

1 Heaven and Earth, or *yang* and *yin*.

2 This poem emphasizes that human action is useless when it opposes one's fate. For a poem with a similar message, see HS 224.

3 This poem refers to the Burning House parable in the Lotus Sutra. Compare with HS 190.

HS 256

可歎浮生人，
悠悠何日了。
朝朝無閑時，
年年不覺老。
總為求衣食，
令心生煩惱。
擾擾百千年，
去來三惡道。

HS 257

時人尋雲路，
雲路杳無蹤。
山高多險峻，
澗闊少玲瓏。
碧嶂前兼後，
白雲西復東。
欲知雲路處，
雲路在虛空。

HS 256

Alas! Those in the floating world—
Into eternity, never ceasing.
Day upon day, no time of rest,
Year after year, not sensing their age.
All in search of clothing and food
Which raises *kleśas* in the mind.
Caught in turmoil for countless years,
Still pacing the Three Evil Paths.

HS 257

People of this age seek a road through the clouds—
But this road is dim and leaves no trace.
The heights of the hill are mostly steep and narrow,
While the ravine is broad with little sunlight.
Emerald cliffs join front to back,
And white clouds drift west and east.
If you wish to know where the cloud-road is:
The cloud-road rests in the empty void.

HS 258

寒山棲隱處，
絕得雜人過。
時逢林內鳥，
相共唱山歌。
瑞草聯谿谷，
老松枕嵯峨。
可觀無事客，
憩歇在巖阿。

HS 259

五嶽俱成粉，
須彌一寸山。
大海一滴水，
吸入在心田。
生長菩提子，
徧蓋天中天。
語汝慕道者，
慎莫繞十纏。

HS 258

I roost in seclusion on Cold Mountain,
Cut off from the calls of distracting men.
At times I encounter birds in the wood,
And together we sing a mountain song.
Auspicious grass stretches through valley and vale;
Old pines lean on looming crags.
There you can see a lodger without affairs,
Taking his ease on the top of a cliff.

HS 259

The Five Sacred Peaks are reduced to powder,
And Mount Sumeru shrinks to an inch.[1]
The great seas are just one drop of water
That is sucked into the field of the mind.
There the seed of the Bodhi tree grows and prospers,
Until it becomes a canopy for the God of the Gods.[2]
I tell those of you who aspire to the Way:
Do not let the Ten Entanglements coil about you.[3]

---

1 The Five Sacred Peaks are five geographically and mythologically significant mountains in the Chinese tradition: Taishan, Hengshan, Huashan, Hengshan, and Songshan. For Mount Sumeru, see HS 119.

2 "The God of the Gods" (天中天) is a term for the Buddha; just as humans honor and respect the gods, so the gods respect the Buddha and take him for their own divinity. Here the Bodhi tree under which the Buddha found enlightenment is also the seeds of enlightenment brought to realization within the human mind.

3 "Entanglements" (纏) is another term for *kleśas*. They are variously defined, but lists include such items as anger, shamelessness, sleepiness, and stinginess.

HS 260

無衣自訪覓，
莫共狐謀裘。
無食自采取，
4 莫共羊謀羞。
借皮兼借肉，
懷歎復懷愁。
皆緣義失所，
8 衣食常不周。

HS 261

自羨山間樂，
逍遙無倚托。
逐日養殘軀，
4 閑思無所作。
時披古佛書，
往往登石閣。
下窺千尺崖，
8 上有雲盤泊。
寒月冷颼颼，
身似孤飛鶴。

HS 260

If you have no clothes, go look for them yourself;
Don't plot to get your robe from the fox.
If you don't have food, go and pick it yourself;
4 Don't plot to take your treats from the lamb.
If they lend their hides, if they lend their flesh,
They'll harbor sighs and harbor grief.
All because justice is misapplied,
8 We are always lacking in clothing and food.

HS 261

I long for the delight of the mountains,
Where I ramble about, depending on nothing.
Day after day I nourish my waning body,
4 Lost in idle thoughts, nothing to do.
Occasionally I leaf through old Buddhist books,
And often climb up the stone walkways.
There I look down from a thousand-foot bluff,
8 While clouds linger over my head.
The winter moon is chilly and windblown,
And my body is like a lone flying crane.

HS 262

我見轉輪王，
千子常圍繞。
十善化四天，
莊嚴多七寶。
七寶鎮隨身，
莊嚴甚妙好。
一朝福報盡，
猶若棲蘆鳥。
還作牛領蟲，
六趣受業道。
況復諸凡夫，
無常豈長保。
生死如旋火，
輪迴似麻稻。
不解早覺悟，
為人枉虛老。

HS 262

I see the Wheel-Turning Kings,[1]
Always surrounded by their thousand sons.
With the Ten Virtues they transform all Four Continents;
Adorned they are with many of the Seven Jewels.[2]
The Seven Jewels accompany them everywhere,
And their adornments are marvelous and fine.
Yet one day their good rewards run out;[3]
They are like birds that roost on a reed.
They'll incarnate as bugs on the neck of an ox;
On the Six Courses they accept their karmic path.
This is even truer for ordinary types;
What can be preserved long amid Impermanence?
Life and death are like spinning flames;[4]
The turning of the wheel like fields of hemp or rice.
If you don't know that you should awaken at once,
You'll waste growing old as a human.[5]

1 Wheel-Turning King: *cakravartin*, a virtuous king who "turns the Wheel of the Dharma" (spreads Buddhism) in the land he rules.

2 The Ten Virtues consist of resisting the Ten Sins: killing, stealing, sexual misconduct, rash talk, hypocritical speech, slander, flattery, greed, anger, and heterodox views. The Four Continents (here described by the poetic phrase "four heavens") are the four continents that make up the habitable world in each Buddhist cosmos. There are various lists for the Seven Jewels (used in Buddhist writing to describe precious things in general).

3 I.e., accumulated good karma from past good deeds (which allowed them to incarnate as Wheel-Turning Kings).

4 "Spinning flame" here is short for "wheel of spinning flame" (旋火輪), an image used in a number of sutras to describe the illusory solidity of human life. When a torch is spun around oneself at night, it creates the illusion of a tangible wheel. The poet may intend an ironic comparison with the Dharma propagated by the Wheel-Turning King (as well as his mention of the karmic wheel of reincarnation at the beginning of the following line).

5 If one is fortunate enough to be born as a human (let alone a Wheel-Turning King), one should strive to attain enlightenment—otherwise, the opportunity is wasted and one may very well fall below humans in the next incarnation.

HS 263

平野水寬闊，
丹丘連四明。
仙都最高秀，
群峰聳翠屏。
遠遠望何極，
矶矶勢相迎。
獨標海隅外，
處處播嘉名。

HS 264

可貴一名山，
七寶何能比。
松月颼颼冷，
雲霞片片起。
匼匝幾重山，
迴還多少里。
谿澗靜澄澄，
快活無窮已。

HS 263

The water stretches far and wide to the plain;
There, Cinnabar Hill rises up to the Four Lights.
Transcendent's Capital is most lofty here,
And the assembled peaks thrust up their emerald screens.[1]
So distant, no end to the vista;
So looming, their forms greet us.
Solitary monuments beyond this remote sea corner,
They broadcast their splendid fame everywhere.

HS 264

Worth treasuring, this famous mountain;
How could a Seven-Jeweled Pagoda compare?[2]
The pine-tree moon is chill and windblown;
The roseate clouds rise, shred by shred.
The many layers of hills, clustered together,
Twist and turn for countless miles.
The valley creeks here are calm and clear;
And my delight never comes to an end.

---

1 These are all names for hills and mountains in the Tiantai range. For Cinnabar Hill, see also HS 195.

2 For the seven jewels, see HS 262.

HS 265

我見世間人，
生而還復死。
昨朝猶二八，
4 壯氣胸襟士。
如今七十過，
力困形憔悴。
恰似春日花，
8 朝開夜落爾。

HS 266

迥聳霄漢外，
雲裏路岧嶢。
瀑布千丈流，
4 如鋪練一條。
下有棲心窟，
橫安定命橋。
雄雄鎮世界，
8 天台名獨超。

HS 265

I see the people of this world;
They live, then return again to death.
Yesterday morn they were still sixteen,
4 Hale and hearty, men of ambition.
And now they're over seventy,
Their strength thwarted and their bodies withered.
They're just like blossoms on a spring day:
8 At dawn they bloom, and by night they fall.

HS 266

It thrusts skyward, beyond Heaven's River;
There in the clouds, the road rises steep.
Waterfalls plunge down a thousand fathoms,
4 Like a stretch of white silk unrolled.
Down there is the Cave of Mind's Rest;
And stretching across is the Bridge of Fate Ordained.[1]
Boldly it bestrides all the world:
8 Tiantai: the name stands alone above all.

1 This is the same stone formation called "Stone Bridge" in HS 44 and HS 218.

HS 267

盤陀石上坐，
谿澗冷淒淒。
靜翫偏嘉麗，
虛巖蒙霧迷。
怡然憩歇處，
日斜樹影低。
我自觀心地，
蓮花出淤泥。

HS 268

隱士遁人間，
多向山中眠。
青蘿疎麓麓，
碧澗響聯聯。
騰騰且安樂，
悠悠自清閑。
免有染世事，
心靜如白蓮。

HS 267

I sit on a broad slab of rock,
Where the valley creek flows cold and brisk.
I calmly take pleasure, only favoring beauty here,
4 Lost in the shrouding mists on this empty cliff.
I joyfully take my rest in this place,
Until the sun sets, casting tree shadows low.
Then I observe the ground of my Mind:
8 A lotus bloom emerging from the muck.

HS 268

When recluses hide from the human world,
Most will sleep in the midst of the hills,
Where green vines grow sparse and distinct,
4 And the deep-blue stream murmurs without end.
In their enthusiasm they take pleasure for a time:
With minds drifting, they grow clear and at ease.
Escaping the worldly affairs that stain,
8 Their minds are as calm as a white lotus.

HS 269

寄語食肉漢，
食時無逗遛。
今生過去種，
未來今日修。
只取今日美，
不畏來生憂。
老鼠入飯瓮，
雖飽難出頭。

HS 270

自從出家後，
漸得養生趣。
伸縮四肢全，
勤聽六根具。
褐衣隨春冬，
糲食供朝暮。
今日懇懇修，
願與佛相遇。

HS 269

I send word to you flesh-eating men,
Who will not cease your eating:
This life had its seeds in your past;
And your futures are cultivated today.
But you only take delight in today,
Not fearing the troubles of your next life.
When a rat enters the rice jar,
He may eat his fill, but he can't get out!

HS 270

Ever since I've "left the household,"
I've developed an interest in nourishing life.
Through yoga I preserve my four limbs;[1]
Through careful effort I perfect my six senses.
I keep a rough robe from spring to winter;
Coarse rice serves me from dawn to dusk.
Today, since I've earnestly practiced,
I'm willing to meet with the Buddhas.

1 "Yoga" translates 伸縮 ("stretching and shrinking"), a term that occurs in early texts to describe different forms of exercise (especially breath control).

HS 271

五言五百篇，
七字七十九。
三字二十一，
都來六百首。
一例書巖石，
自誇云好手。
若能會我詩，
真是如來母。

HS 272

世事繞悠悠，
貪生早晚休。
研盡大地石，
何時得歇頭。
四時周變易，
八節急如流。
為報火宅主，
露地騎白牛。

HS 271

Pentasyllabic pieces, five hundred;
Heptasyllabics, seventy-nine;
Trisyllabics, twenty-one:
All together, six hundred poems.
All of them written on cliff rocks:
I boast I've got a good hand!
And if you can understand them,
That's the basis for becoming a Tathāgata.[1]

HS 272

The affairs of the world entwine us forever;
When will this greed for life ever end?
Grind away at an enormous rock:
When will such labors cease?
The four seasons circle about in their change;
The eight nodes pass swift as flowing water.[2]
That's why I tell the masters of the burning house:
Go ride your white ox in the open air!

1 Though many scholars have cited this poem as evidence that the HS collection was once twice its current size, it would be rash to base such an assumption on this poem alone, considering the likelihood of multiple authorship. Also, the arrangement of numbers here to fit the rhyme and rhythm of the poem seems a bit too pat to reflect reality.

2 Another way of indicating the cycle of the year; the eight nodes are the two solstices, the two equinoxes, and the first day of each of the four seasons.

HS 273

可笑五陰窟，
四蛇同共居。
黑暗無明燭，
三毒遞相驅。
伴黨六箇賊，
劫掠法財珠。
斬却魔軍輩，
安泰湛如蘇。

HS 274

常聞漢武帝，
爰及秦始皇。
俱好神仙術，
延年竟不長。
金臺既摧折，
沙丘遂滅亡。
茂陵與驪嶽，
今日草茫茫。

HS 273

What a laugh, this cave of the Five Skandhas,
Where the Four Snakes live together![1]
All is blackness there, without a lit candle;
The Three Poisons chase each other in and out.[2]
They band together with the Six Thieves,[3]
To plunder and loot the Dharma's treasure jewels.
But if you behead this demon army,
It will bring peace, as calming as clotted cream.[4]

HS 274

I've often heard of Emperor Wu of the Han,
As well as the first Qin emperor.
Both of them were fond of Transcendent arts,
Yet in the end their lives were not prolonged.[5]
Now the gold terraces are shattered and broken,
And Sandhill has vanished away.[6]
At Maoling and at Li Peak[7]
Today the weeds grow thick.

---

1 For skandhas, see HS 202. The "cave" here is the Self. The Four Snakes are the four physical elements that compose the body: earth, water, fire, and wind (see also HS 249).

2 The Three Poisons are: desire, anger, and ignorance. See also HS 91 and HS 226.

3 The six senses. See also HS 244 and HS 249.

4 蘇 here is used for 酥; clotted cream is mentioned in the sutras as a metaphor for the soothing teaching of the Dharma.

5 Both rulers were infamous in their desire to find the secret of immortality.

6 Gold terraces: a general reference to structures built by Han Wudi meant to be used in communication with Transcendents. Sandhill was the site of the first Qin emperor's death.

7 The sites of the tombs of Emperor Wu and the first Qin emperor respectively.

HS 275

憶得二十年,
徐步國清歸。
國清寺中人,
盡道寒山癡。
癡人何用疑,
疑不解尋思。
我尚自不識,
是伊爭得知。
低頭不用問,
問得復何為。
有人來罵我,
分明了了知。
雖然不應對,
却是得便宜。

HS 276

語你出家輩,
何名為出家。
奢華求養活,
繼綴族姓家。
美舌甜脣觜,
諂曲心鉤加。

HS 275

I remember twenty years ago,
When I took my leisured way back to Guoqing Temple.
The men at Guoqing Temple
All said that I, Hanshan, was a fool.
But what use is there to suspect a fool?
They suspect he won't understand how to think.
But if I myself don't understand,
Then how would *they* be able to know?
I kept my head low—useless to ask questions;
For why would I want to ask questions?
Then people came to scold me,
And I clearly understood at once.
And though I didn't reply to them,
I did find something to my advantage.

HS 276

I ask you now, who have "left the home":
What does it mean to leave the home?
You seek to feed your wealthy lives
And find ways to keep your clan intact:
With pretty tongues and honeyed lips,
With flattery and crooked hearts.

終日禮道場，
持經置功課。
鑪燒神佛香，
打鐘高聲和。
六時學客舂，
晝夜不得臥。
只為愛錢財，
心中不脫灑。
見他高道人，
却嫌誹謗罵。
驢屎比麝香，
苦哉佛陀耶。

HS 277

又見出家兒，
有力及無力。
上上高節者，
鬼神欽道德。
君王分輦坐，
諸侯拜迎逆。
堪為世福田，
世人須保惜。

All day you pray in the Buddha Hall,
Grasp sutras for your daily chant.
Burn incense fit for Buddhas and gods,
Strike the bells with their high harmonies.
Acting all day like a hired hand,[1]
Not a moment's rest from day to night.
But just because you covet wealth,
You can't escape it in your mind.
Then when you see some lofty monk,
You doubt him and malign and curse.
Ass dung next to the finest musk:
Oh Buddha! How bitter it all is.

HS 277

I've also seen those who leave the household,
Both those with ability and those without.
The best of the best, with lofty self-restraint:
Ghosts and spirits respect their virtue.
Lords and princes grant them seats in their palanquins,
And feudal lords respectfully receive them.
They are worth becoming the age's Field of Blessings,
And people of the age should all treasure them.

1 Literally, "through the six periods of the day imitating a hired laborer pounding grain." The point here is that the monk is not doing these rituals for his own salvation or out of compassion for sentient beings, but merely because he has been employed to do them by donors to the temple.

下下低愚者，
詐現多求覓。
濁濫即可知，
愚癡愛財色。
著却福田衣，
種田討衣食。
作債稅牛犁，
為事不忠直。
朝朝行弊惡，
往往痛臀脊。
不解善思量，
地獄惡無極。
一朝著病纏，
三年臥床席。
亦有真佛性，
翻作無明賊。
南無佛陀耶，
遠遠求彌勒。

The lowest of the low, most stupid of all:
They make false display, mostly in search of gain.
Their polluted natures may be known;
In their foolishness they're fond of wealth and sex.
Though they wear the robe of the Blessing Field,[1]
They plant fields seeking clothing and food.
They lend money, rent out ox and plow,
Faithless and false in what they do.
Every day they practice their wickedness,
And they are constantly flogged for their acts.[2]
They don't know how to think good and hard
That hell is awful and limitless.
One day you might be caught in the bonds of illness,
And for three years must lie on your bed and mat.[3]
Indeed, they have the nature of a true Buddha,
But instead they act like ignorant robbers.
All hail the Lord Buddha!
May we all seek Maitreya afar.[4]

1 I.e., a monk's robe. For Field of Blessings, see HS 233.

2 Literally, "constantly sore on the buttocks and spine."

3 Illness here is a comparative metaphor: just as a moment of contagion may result in a lengthy illness, one bad action may have severe karmic consequences.

4 I interpret this final couplet as a sort of "benediction" to the poem.

HS 278

寒巖深更好，
無人行此道。
白雲高岫閑，
青嶂孤猨嘯。
我更何所親，
暢志自宜老。
形容寒暑遷，
心珠甚可保。

HS 279

巖前獨靜坐，
圓月當天耀。
萬象影現中，
一輪本無照。
廓然神自清，
含虛洞玄妙。
因指見其月，
月是心樞要。

HS 278

It's better that Cold Cliff is remote;
Then no one will travel the road here.
White clouds idly drift by high peaks,
And solitary gibbons howl on green cliffs.
I no longer take anyone as my friends;
With my will indulged, it's the best way to grow old.
Though my form may alter with the cold and heat,
I can really protect the jewel of my mind.

HS 279

In front of the cliff I sit quietly and alone;
The full moon sparkles in the sky.
The shadows of everything appear in its light,
And yet its single wheel does not shine on its own.
It is expansive, its spirit naturally clear;
Transparent it is, hollow, a mysterious marvel.
See this moon as I point at it!
The moon is the pivot of the mind.

HS 280

本志慕道倫，
道倫常獲親。
時逢杜源客，
每接話禪賓。
談玄月明夜，
探理日臨晨。
萬機俱泯跡，
方識本來人。

HS 281

元非隱逸士，
自號山林人。
仕魯蒙幘帛，
且愛裹疎巾。
道有巢許操，
耻為堯舜臣。
獼猴罩帽子，
學人避風塵。

HS 280

My aspirations admire these companions of the Way;
Companions of the Way, whom I always befriend.
At times I meet a wanderer who has stopped up the source,[1]
And I always greet a guest who speaks of meditation.
We chat of mysteries on nights of bright moon,
And investigate principle until the sun rises.
When all the concerns of the world vanish with their traces,
Only then we know the original Self.

HS 281

Basically not even recluses at all,
They call themselves "men of the mountain woods."
They work for the state, accept the official's head cloth,[2]
But wrap themselves in the hermit's turban.[3]
They say they've the virtue of Chao or Xu,
Are ashamed to act as Yao's or Shun's statesmen.[4]
But they're monkeys wearing people hats,
Aping humans who shun the windblown dust.

---

1 That is, no longer acts in such a way as to produce karma (either good or bad). This is sometimes described as having "no outflows" (*wu lou*). Compare HS 303.

2 "Work for the state" here is literally "act as ministers for Lu," the ancient Chinese state associated with Confucius.

3 The "hermit's turban" was a headgear associated with rich scholars presuming to play the role of the retired gentleman, common from the fourth century CE on.

4 Chao Fu 巢父 and Xu You 許由 were both legendary recluses who figure in early Daoist folklore; both of them were offered the throne of the empire by the ancient sage-king Yao and both refused it, citing their desire to remain free of the pollution of public office. Yao then passed the throne on to the virtuous Shun.

HS 282

自古諸哲人，
不見有長存。
生而還復死，
盡變作灰塵。
積骨如毗富，
別淚成海津。
唯有空名在，
豈免生死輪。

HS 283

今日巖前坐，
坐久煙雲收。
一道清谿冷，
千尋碧嶂頭。
白雲朝影靜，
明月夜光浮。
身上無塵垢，
心中那更憂。

HS 282

From olden times, all the wise men:
I've never seen one who could remain forever.
They live, then return again to death,
All transformed to ash and dust.
A pile of bones high as Mount Vipula,[1]
Tears of parting become a sea.
Only their empty fame remains—
They could not avoid the wheel of rebirth.

HS 283

Today I am siting before the cliff,
Sitting long until the mist and clouds withdraw.
One stretch of clear creek, cold;
A thousand fathoms of emerald cliff.
The morning shadow of the white clouds is quiet,
The nocturnal light of the bright moon floats.
No filth at all is on my body—
What more should worry me in my heart?

1 For Mount Vipula, see HS 233.

HS 284

千雲萬水間，
中有一閑士。
白日遊青山，
夜歸巖下睡。
倏爾過春秋，
寂然無塵累。
快哉何所依，
靜若秋江水。

HS 285

勸你休去來，
莫惱他閻老。
失脚入三途，
粉骨遭千擣。
長為地獄人，
永隔今生道。
勉你信余言，
識取衣中寶。

HS 284

Mid a thousand clouds and a myriad waters,
There is an idle gentleman.
In daylight he roams the green hills,
Returning at night to sleep at the cliff's foot.
In a flash he passes through spring and autumn;
He is serene, unencumbered by dusty ties.
Delightful! He depends on nothing;
He is as tranquil as an autumn river.

HS 285

I urge you to cease your coming and going—
Don't aggravate Old Man Yama![1]
One slip and you've entered the Three Evil Paths,
Flogged a thousand times, your bones ground to powder.
You'll long remain a denizen of Hell,
Forever cut off from the course you now live.
I press you to believe my words,
And recognize the jewel in your robe.[2]

1 The king of Hell/the Underworld.

2 This is an allusion to a parable in the Lotus Sutra, in which a man endures much poverty and suffering without realizing that his friend has sewn a jewel in his clothes. The jewel stands for the Buddha Nature. As with many of the Hanshan poems, this one emphasizes that only sudden realization of the Buddha Nature will allow one to escape the cycles of rebirth, which sooner or later will result in an existence in the hell realms.

HS 286

世間一等流，
誠堪與人笑。
出家弊己身，
4 誑俗將為道。
雖著離塵衣，
衣中多養蚤。
不如歸去來，
8 識取心王好。

HS 287

高高峰頂上，
四顧極無邊。
獨坐無人知，
4 孤月照寒泉。
泉中且無月，
月自在青天。
吟此一曲歌，
8 歌終不是禪。

HS 286

There's a kind of person in the world
Who really has to make you laugh.
He "leaves the home," brings harm to self;
To con the people is his Way.
Though he wears the garb that transcends dust,[1]
His garb is the breeding ground for fleas.
Better far just to go back home,
Discern the virtue of the Prince of the Mind.

HS 287

High up above, on the top of the peak,
I can see all around without limit.
I sit solitary, and no one knows I am here—
While a lone moon shines on the cold stream.
But there is no moon in the stream itself—
The moon is actually in the night sky.
And when I chant this single song,
There is no *dhyāna* when the song ends.[2]

1 I.e., a monk's robe.

2 Just as the reflection of the moon should not be mistaken for the moon itself, so the poem should not be confused for the act of meditation (*dhyāna*) itself.

HS 288

有箇王秀才，
笑我詩多失。
云不識蜂腰，
仍不會鶴膝。
平側不解壓，
凡言取次出。
我笑你作詩，
如盲徒詠日。

HS 289

我住在村鄉，
無爺亦無娘。
無名無姓第，
人喚作張王。
並無人教我，
貧賤也尋常。
自憐心的實，
堅固等金剛。

HS 288

A certain Wang, examinee—
He laughs at all my metric flaws.
He says, "You don't know Wasp-Waist,
4 And fail to notice Crane-knee faults.
You can't deploy the level and slant,
And you scatter slang just everywhere."[1]
But I chuckle when *you* write verse—
8 A blind man trying to praise the sun.

HS 289

I live in a country village,
Without a dad, and without a mom,
No name, no surname or family rank;
4 People just call me "Zhang" or "Wang."
And no one has ever taught me;
I'm poor and lowly and ordinary.
But I cherish the reality of my Mind;
8 It's as firm as diamond.

1 These are all errors in diction and tonality that were considered anathema in the recently developed "regulated verse" (*lü shi* 律詩) of the Tang era (the elite verse form *par excellence*).

HS 290

寒山出此語，
此語無人信。
蜜甜足人嘗，
黃蘗苦難近。
順情生喜悅，
逆意多瞋恨。
但看木傀儡，
弄了一場困。

HS 291

我見人轉經，
依他言語會。
口轉心不轉，
心口相違背。
心真無委曲，
不作諸纏蓋。
但且自省躬，
莫覓他替代。
可中作得主，
是知無內外。

HS 290

Hanshan utters these words—
These words that no one believes.
Honey is sweet enough for people to taste,
But Amur cork is too bitter to try.[1]
If you follow their mood, they're happy and delighted;
Go against their will, and most grow angry and resentful.
Just look at those wooden puppets,
Acting out their performance of hardship!

HS 291

I see people "turning sutras":[2]
They depend on others' words to understand.
Their mouths will turn, but not their minds,
So minds and mouths go different ways.
If your mind's true and has no twist,
You won't create entangling blocks.
So just be sure to watch yourself,
And don't look for others to take your place.
For if you learn to act as master,
This knowledge will have no "in" or "out."

1 For Amur cork, see HS 125.

2 "Turning sutras" (*zhuan jing*) is an idiomatic term for reading sutras aloud (often in a ceremonial capacity).

HS 292

寒山唯白雲，
寂寂絕埃塵。
草座山家有，
孤燈明月輪。
石床臨碧沼，
虎鹿每為鄰。
自羨幽居樂，
長為象外人。

HS 293

鹿生深林中，
飲水而食草。
伸脚樹下眠，
可憐無煩惱。
繫之在華堂，
餚膳極肥好。
終日不肯嘗，
形容轉枯槁。

HS 292

Only white clouds at Cold Mountain;
Tranquil, severed from dust and grime.
My mountain home has seats of woven grass;
The bright moon's wheel is my only lamp.
My stone bench looks down on the deep blue pond;
Tigers and deer are always my neighbors.
I long for the joy of my hidden dwelling;
I'll always dwell beyond the world of forms.

HS 293

A deer was born in the deep forest,
Where he drank the water and ate the grass.
He would stretch his legs and sleep under the trees;
A life to cherish, without nuisances.
Then they tied him up at a splendid hall,
Fed him rare delicacies, lovely and fine.
All day he is unwilling to eat,
And his body grows ever more gaunt.

HS 294

花上黃鶯子，
喧喧聲可憐。
美人顏似玉，
對此弄鳴弦。
翫之能不足，
眷戀在齠年。
花飛鳥亦散，
灑淚秋風前。

HS 295

棲遲寒巖下，
偏訝最幽奇。
攜籃采山茹，
挈籠摘果歸。
蔬齋敷茅坐，
啜啄食紫芝。
清沼濯瓢鉢，
雜和煑稠稀。
當陽擁裘坐，
閑讀古人詩。

HS 294

The yellow orioles on the flowers
Twitter with a charming sound.
A beauty with a face like jade
Faces them as she toys with her sounding strings.
She is more than willing to play with them—
But these were dearest childhood loves.
The flowers fly away and the birds leave too—
She spills her tears in the autumn wind.

HS 295

I roost and roam at the foot of Cold Cliff,
Especially amazed at its most hidden marvels.
I took hamper in hand and picked mountain vegetables,
I brought a basket and returned with fruit.
Now in my simple lodging I spread rushes and sit;
I chew on the purple mushrooms,
Then wash gourd and bowl in a clear pool,
As I blend and simmer the thick and the thin.
Basking in the sun I sit with my robe about me,
Idly reading the poetry of the men of old.

HS 296

昔日經行處，
今復七十年。
故人無來往，
4 埋在古冢間。
余今頭已白，
猶守片雲山。
為報後來子，
8 何不讀古言。

HS 297

欲向東巖去，
于今無量年。
昨來攀葛上，
4 半路困風煙。
徑窄衣難進，
苔粘履不前。
住兹丹桂下，
8 且枕白雲眠。

HS 296

The places I visited in former days—
Now seventy years ago.
No more do old friends frequent me;
They're buried now in old tomb mounds.
And now my head's already white
While I still keep to this cloud-shred of hill.
That is why I tell those who will come after me:
Why not read these words of old?

HS 297

I've wanted to go to East Mountain
For countless years till now.
Yesterday I clambered up vines,
But wind and mist blocked me halfway.
Hard for clothes to brave the narrow path,
And clinging moss hampered my shoes.
So halting beneath an osmanthus tree,
I slept a while, with white clouds for my pillow.

HS 298

我見利智人，
觀者便知意。
不假尋文字，
4 直入如來地。
心不逐諸緣，
意根不妄起。
心意不生時，
8 內外無餘事。

HS 299

身著空花衣，
足躡龜毛履。
手把兔角弓，
擬射無明鬼。

HS 300

君看葉裏花，
能得幾時好。
今日畏人攀，
4 明朝待誰掃。

HS 298

I see those men, clever and wise;
Observe them, then you'll know their thoughts.
They don't rely on a search for written words,
4 But enter directly the Tathāgata's ground.
If your mind doesn't chase after the various conditions,
Then the thinking sense will not wildly arise.
And if mind and thinking do not come into being,
8 There will be nothing remaining within and without.

HS 299

I don clothes fashioned of illusion,
And tread in shoes made of tortoise fur.
In my hand I grasp a bow of rabbit horn,
Planning to shoot the demons of ignorance.

HS 300

You've seen blossoms amid the leaves:
How long will they remain fine?
Today I fear someone will pluck them;
4 Tomorrow I'll wait for them to be swept away.

可憐嬌豔情，
年多轉成老。
將世比於花，
8 紅顏豈長保。

HS 301

桂棟非吾宅，
松林是我家。
一生俄爾過，
4 萬事莫言賒。
濟渡不造筏，
漂淪為采花。
善根今未種，
8 何日見生芽。

HS 302

出生三十年，
當遊千萬里。
行江青草合，
4 入塞紅塵起。

Lovely, this charming, seductive mood—
But with the years we grow older and older.
Compare this world with these flowers—
How can a rosy face last forever?

HS 301

Rafters of cinnamon wood—that's not my house;
The pine tree forest—*that's* my home.
A single life passes in an instant;
Don't say that worldly affairs are slow to come.
If you're not building a raft to cross the river,
Then you'll drift away because you picked flowers.[1]
If you don't plant the roots of good deeds now,
When will you ever see the sprouts emerge?

HS 302

I've been in the world for thirty years
And I must have traveled a million miles.
Walked by rivers where the green grass grows thick,
And entered the frontier where the red dust rises.

1 That is, if you aren't intent on crossing the river (attaining salvation), you might dawdle in ordinary pleasures and find yourself carried off by the current of samsara.

鍊藥空求仙，
讀書兼詠史。
今日歸寒山，
枕流兼洗耳。

HS 303

寒山無漏巖，
其巖甚濟要。
八風吹不動，
萬古人傳妙。
寂寂好安居，
空空離譏誚。
孤月夜長明，
圓日常來照。
虎丘兼虎谿，
不用相呼召。
世間有王傅，
莫把同周邵。
我自遯寒巖，
快活長歌笑。

Purified potions in vain search for immortality,
Read books and perused the histories.
Today I return to Cold Mountain,
8 Pillow myself on the creek and wash out my ears.

HS 303

Cold Mountain is a cliff with no outflows;[1]
This cliff is a must if you would be saved.
It stays motionless amid the Eight Winds,[2]
4 And people have told of its marvels forever.
So tranquil: a fine place to dwell at peace.
So empty: away from mockery and contempt.
The lonely moon at night is ever bright;
8 The round sun always comes to shine.
Tiger Hill and Tiger Valley—[3]
No point in inviting me *there*.
In the world, one may be tutor to princes;
12 But there's no way to rank with Zhou or Shao.[4]
I shall betake myself to Cold Cliff,
Where I will be happy, forever singing and laughing.

1 "No outflows" refers to the condition of someone who no longer produces new karmic causes and conditions when she/he acts. The line here suggests that those who cultivate practice on Cold Mountain will no longer generate karma.

2 The Eight Winds are the various forces that can stimulate emotion: gain, loss, slander, eulogy, praise, ridicule, sorrow, and joy.

3 Two scenic spots: Tiger Hill is in Suzhou, and Tiger Valley at Mount Lu.

4 Since the Duke of Zhou and the Duke of Shao were both famed for tutoring King Cheng of Zhou in his rule, they are examples of virtuous ministers that the speaker cannot hope to emulate. Better instead to become a recluse.

HS 304

沙門不持戒，
道士不服藥。
自古多少賢，
盡在青山脚。

HS 305

有人笑我詩，
我詩合典雅。
不煩鄭氏箋，
豈用毛公解。
不恨會人稀，
只為知音寡。
若遣趁宮商，
余病莫能罷。
忽遇明眼人，
即自流天下。

HS 304

A monk who will not keep the precepts;
A Daoist who does not take drugs.
Since times gone by, so many worthy men
Have ended below the green hills.[1]

HS 305

There are people who laugh at my poems;
Yet my poems are in keeping with the classic odes.
But you needn't bother with Master Zheng's notes,
Nor use the explanations of Lord Mao.[2]
I don't resent that those who understand are rare;
It's only because those who know me are few.
I have resigned chasing after *gong* and *shang*,
And I can't give up my metric flaws.[3]
But if they meet up with a clear-sighted person,
They'll be propagated throughout the world.

1 If you do not take your religious practice seriously, you will neither become a Transcendent (if a Daoist) or escape the cycles of rebirth (if Buddhist), and will simply perish, as many worthy ones have done in the past.

2 The poet is comparing his verse to the Classic of Poetry (*Shijing*), but saying that they are easier to understand, without need of commentary (Zheng and Mao were standard commentaries on the classic).

3 This is a tentative translation of an obscure couplet. I take it to mean that the poet does not follow the rules of tonal regulation (宮 and 商 are musical modes used sometimes to describe the tones of verse prosody), and that he does not plan to reform (病 is used specifically to refer to violations of tonal propriety). Cf. HS 286 for another defense of metrical violation.

HS 306

寒山道，
無人到。
若能行，
稱十號。
有蟬鳴，
無鴉噪。
黃葉落，
白雲掃。
石磊磊，
山隩隩。
我獨居，
名善導。
子細看，
何相好。

HS 307

寒山寒，
冰鎖石。
藏山青，
現雪白。

HS 306

The Cold Mountain road:
No one comes.
If you're able to travel it,
You'll be called by ten names.[1]
There cicadas cry,
But no crows caw.
Yellow leaves fall,
And white clouds sweep.
Stones are heaped,
The mountain is remote.
I dwell here alone;
I am named "Good Guide."[2]
But if you look carefully,
What attributes do I have?[3]

HS 307

Cold Mountain is cold;
Ice locks in the rocks,
Hides the mountain's green,
Reveals the white of snow.

1 I.e., become a Buddha. These refer to ten honorific titles granted to the Buddha.

2 One of the titles of the Buddha.

3 "Attributes" (相) can be applied to the list of special physical qualities that the Buddha is said to possess; however, Mahayana thought (e.g., the Diamond Sutra) asserts that Buddhas are not knowable by their attributes. This poem may allude specifically to the preface, in which Fenggan mysteriously hinted that Hanshan would not be recognizable in his incarnation as Mañjuśrī.

日出照，
一時釋。
從茲暖，
8 養老客。

HS 308

我居山，
勿人識。
白雲中，
常寂寂。

HS 309

寒山深，
稱我心。
純白石，
4 勿黃金。
泉聲響，
撫伯琴。
有子期，
8 辨此音。

But the sun comes out to shine,
And all at once it thaws.
From then on, it's warm,
And can sustain an old man.

HS 308

I live on the mountain,
And no one knows me.
Amid the white clouds
It's always tranquil.

HS 309

Cold Mountain is deep;
This pleases my mind.
Purely white stone,
And no yellow gold.
The streams resound
As I strum Bo Ya's zither.
If Ziqi were here,
He could distinguish the notes.[1]

1 A reference to the famous story of the great zither player Bo Ya, whose music was appreciated and understood by his close friend Zhongzi Qi.

HS 310

重巖中，
足清風。
扇不搖，
涼冷通。
明月照，
白雲籠。
獨自坐，
一老翁。

HS 311

寒山子，
長如是。
獨自居，
不生死。

HS 310

In the layered cliffs,
There is enough clear breeze.
No fan gets waved,
Yet fresh coolness arrives.
The bright moon shines,
Encircled in white clouds.
Alone I sit,
One old man.

HS 311

Master Hanshan
Is always like this.
He dwells alone,
Neither is born nor dies.[1]

1 I.e., now free from the cycle of rebirth.

拾遺二首新添

HS 312

我見世間人，
箇箇爭意氣。
一朝忽然死，
只得一片地。
闊四尺，
長丈二。
汝若會出來爭意氣，
我與汝立碑記。

HS 313

家有寒山詩，
勝汝看經卷。
書放屏風上，
時時看一遍。

已上詩除拾遺二首老僧相傳其外。切依古印本排比次第耳。

I have newly added these two recovered poems:

HS 312

I see the people of the world:
Each with their competitive minds.
Then one day they suddenly die,
And get only one plot of land.
Four feet wide,
Twelve feet long.
If you can fathom their competitive minds,
Then I'll erect a stele in your honor.

HS 313

If your house has Hanshan's poems,
That's better than reading the sutras.
Write them down on a screen,
And read one now and then.

All of the poems above (except for the two poems discovered later that I have transmitted) have been put in sequence based on comparisons with old printed editions.[1]

1 This note in the Song Edition (probably printed some time between 1120 and 1170) testifies to the existence of earlier printed editions, though none have survived. The editor refers to himself as *lao seng* ("old monk").

豐干禪師錄

道者豐干。未窮根裔。古老見之。居于天台山國清寺。翦髮齊眉。毳裘擁質。緇素問鞠。乃云隨時。貌悴昂藏。恢端七尺。

唯攻舂米供僧。夜則扃房。吟詠自樂。郡縣諳知。咸謂風僧。或發一言。異於常流。忽爾一日。騎虎松徑。來入國清。巡廊唱道。眾皆驚訝。怕懼惶然。並欽其德。

昔京輦與胤救疾。到任丹丘。跡無追訪。賢人隱遯。示化東甌。唯於房中壁上書曰。

FG 1

余自來天台，
凡經幾萬迴。
一身如雲水，
悠悠任去來。

逍遙絕無鬧，
忘機隆佛道。

DOI 10.1515/9781501501913-007,

Record of Meditation Master Fenggan[1]

No one has determined the ancestry of the Buddhist practitioner Fenggan. According to the view of elders in the area, he resided at the Guoqing Temple in the Tiantai Mountains. He cut his hair level with his eyebrows, and wrapped himself in a woolly robe. Whenever monks or laypeople made inquiries of him, he'd just say "It all depends." He was haggard in appearance, but dignified and imposing, seven feet in height.

His only task was to grind grain for offerings. At night he would bar the door to his room, then sing and chant to amuse himself. The people of the district knew him well, and took him to be mad. But sometimes he would utter something quite out of the ordinary. One day he showed up riding a tiger along the path through the pine trees and into the temple grounds. He circled about the temple galleries singing; everyone was terrified, but they all admired his moral authority.

In the past, he cured me of an illness when I was in the capital; but when I arrived at my office at Cinnabar Hill [the Tiantai district], I could find no trace of him. He was a worthy who had hidden himself, manifesting himself magically in the region of eastern Ou.[2] There were only some lines written on the walls of his room:[3]

FG 1

Ever since I came to Tiantai
Myriads of cycles have gone by.
My single form is like cloud and water,
And through the vastness I go where I please.

Free and easy, with no annoyances,
I forget concerns while enlarging the Buddha's path.

1 This note is supposedly written by Lüqiu Yin, the purported author of the Preface.
2 Ou 甌 is an early name for the coastal area of Zhejiang where the Tiantai Mountains are located.
3 The Song Edition prints the first poem in a format separate from the second poem. The first poem is twenty lines long, divided by stanza divisions indicated by rhyme change. The second poem is a short quatrain in *gātha* style.

世途歧路心，
眾生多煩惱。

兀兀沈浪海，
漂漂輪三界。
可惜一靈物，
無始被境埋。
電光瞥然起，
生死紛塵埃。
寒山特相訪，
拾得罕期來。
論心話明月，
太虛廓無礙。
法界即無邊，
一法普徧該。

FG 2

本來無一物，
亦無塵可拂。
若能了達此，
不用坐兀兀。

The roads of the world, the crossroads-mind—
Sentient beings have so many annoyances:

Stupefied, lost in the wave-tossed sea,
Drifting along on the Three Realms' wheel.
What a pity that this numinous thing[1]
Since before time has been buried in sensory realms.
A lightning flash like the blink of an eye;
Life and death a scattering of dust.
Hanshan visits me especially,
And Shide comes on rare occasions.
We discuss the mind, speak of the bright moon;
An empty void, broad, without obstruction.
The dharmadhātu has no borders—
One Dharma that encompasses all things.[2]

FG 2

Originally there is not a single thing
Nor any dust to be brushed off.
If you are able to penetrate this completely,
Then no use to sit there like a lump.[3]

1 The Buddha Nature. Compare with HS 179.

2 Dharmadhātu ("realm of reality") refers to various planes of existence, including the Six Courses.

3 A flash of true understanding is superior to empty meditation.

拾得錄

豐干禪師寒山拾得者。在唐太宗貞觀年中。相次垂跡於國清寺。

拾得者。豐干禪師因遊松徑。徐步於赤城道路側。偶而聞啼。乃尋其由。見一子。可年十歲。初謂彼村牧牛之子。委問逗遛。云。我無舍無姓。遂引至寺。付庫院。候人來認。數旬之間。絕其親鞠。乃令事知庫僧靈熠。經于三祀。頗會人言。令知食堂香燈供養。

忽於一日。與像對坐。佛盤同餐。復于聖僧前云。小果之位。喃喃呵俚。而言傷哉。熠謂老宿等。此子心風。無令下供養。乃令厨內洗濾器物。每澄食滓。而以筒盛。寒山子來。負之而去。或發一言。我有一珠。埋在陰中。無人別者。眾謂癡子。

DOI 10.1515/9781501501913-008,

Record of Shide

The Meditation Master Fenggan, as well as Hanshan and Shide, all manifested themselves in turn at the Guoqing Temple during the Zhenguan era of Emperor Taizong of the Tang [627–649].

As for Shide: Meditation Master Fenggan was once traveling on a path through a grove of pine trees, strolling along a way that ran by the side of Redwall. He happened to hear the sound of crying. When he went to investigate, he found a child about ten years old. At first he assumed it to be the son of a herdsman of the local village. When he paused to question the lad, the lad replied: "I have neither home nor surname." Fenggan then brought him back to the temple, where he was attached to the storehouse compounds.[1] They waited for someone to claim him. After several weeks had passed, they gave up trying to locate his relations. He was then sent to serve Lingyi, the monk in charge of the storehouse. After three years had gone by and he could understand the words of others rather well, he was put in charge of looking after the offerings made for the incense lamps in the refectory.

One day he was found sitting in front of the images, eating out of the offering trays. Then he moved back in front of the Holy Monk statues[2] and was heard to mutter, "a lesser stage of attainment . . ." and then, "Your teachings are harmful!" Lingyi told the senior monks that the boy was mad and should not be allowed to present offerings. So he was sent to the refectory kitchen, where he was put to washing dishes. Whenever he was rinsing off the leftovers, he would place them in a bamboo tube. Master Hanshan would take it with him whenever he came. Once the boy said out loud, "I have a jewel buried in a hidden place, but no one can tell it is there!"[3] Everyone thought he was a fool.

1 This anecdote accounts for the monk's name, Shide ("foundling").

2 The images here are referred to as 聖僧 ("holy monks"), a term used to describe the statues in the temple refectory to whom sacrifices are made. They usually represented major bodhisattvas.

3 I suspect there is a pun here, playing on the character *yin* 陰, which can refer to the *skandha*, but may also refer to the genitalia. In that case, this is an obscene version of the Buddha-Nature jewel metaphor (seen for example in HS 202).

寺內山王。僧常參奉。及下供養香燈等務。食物多被烏所耗。忽一夜。僧眾同夢見山王云。拾得打我。瞋云。汝是神道。守護伽藍。更受沙門參奉供養。既有靈驗。何以食被烏殘。今後不要僧參奉供養。至旦。僧眾上堂。各說所夢。皆無一差。靈熠亦然。

喧喧未止。熠下供養。忽見山王身上。而有杖痕所損。熠乃報眾。眾皆奔看。各云夜夢斯事。乃知拾得不是凡間之子。一寺紛紜。具狀申州報縣。符下。賢士遯跡。菩薩化身。宜令號為拾得賢士。「自此後常使淨人直香火供養。」

There was an image of the mountain god in the temple, and the monks would always present it with offerings. After they had made them, had burnt incense, and had carried out other duties, the food would often be consumed by crows. One night, the assembly monks all had the same dream. The mountain god appeared to them and said, "Shide has given me a beating! He glared at me and said, 'You are a god, and you protect this temple. Besides, you receive offerings from all of the monks. Since you have supernatural powers, how can you eat what the crows leave behind?' From now on don't offer me anything." When dawn came, and the monks assembled in the hall, each of them told what he had dreamed. It was the same in every particular. Lingyi as well had had an identical dream.

Before the hubbub could subside, Lingyi went in to make his offerings, and he suddenly noticed that there were gouges in the statue of the mountain god that had been made by a staff. He reported this to the assembly, and they all hurried in to see. They all agreed that since they had all dreamed of this the previous night, they knew that Shide was not an ordinary lad. The whole temple was thrown into confusion. They reported the matter in detail to both the county and the district. They then received a directive, saying that Shide was a Worthy concealing his traces, in fact a bodhisattva's avatar; and that it was fitting that he be called the Honorable Shide. (Note: From this time on, lay stewards have always been sent to set out the incense offerings.)

又於莊頭牧牛。歌詠叫天。又因半月布薩。眾僧說戒。法事合時。拾得驅牛至堂前。倚門而立。撫掌微笑曰。悠悠哉。聚頭作相。這箇如何。老宿律德怒而呵云。下人風狂。破於說戒。拾得笑而言曰。無瞋即是戒。心淨即出家。我性與汝合。一切法無差。尊宿出堂打趂拾得。令驅牛出去。拾得言。我不放牛也。此群牛皆是前生大德知事人。咸有法號。喚者皆認。時拾得一一喚牛云。前生律師弘靖出。時一白牛作聲而過。又喚。前生典座光超出。時一黑牛作聲而過。又喚。直歲靖本出。時一牯牛作聲而出。又喚云。前生知事法忠出。時一牯牛作聲而出。乃獨牽謂牛曰。前生不持戒。人面而畜心。汝今招此咎。怨恨於何人。佛力雖然大。汝辜於佛恩。

He would also look after the oxen on the temple estate, when he would sing and shout to the sky above. One time, during the fortnightly retreat when the monks came together in a service to hear the Precepts, Shide drove the oxen to the front of the hall just as the ceremony was drawing to a close. He stood there leaning against a gate, clapping his hands and smiling. "How common, this way you continue to produce the marks of existence? What's up with that?"[1] The Venerable Lüde grew angry and shouted at him. "You lowborn maniac! You've interrupted the reading of the precepts!" Shide laughed. "Not getting angry is actually a precept, and keeping the mind pure is the same as becoming a monk. My nature is the same as yours! There isn't the slightest difference in our dharma." The Venerable came out of the hall to drive him off and to make him lead the oxen away. But Shide said, "I'm not the one who let the oxen out. Rather, they were all men of great virtue and wisdom in their previous lives. All of them have dharma names—if you call them out, they'll acknowledge them!" Shide then called out to the oxen one by one: "Past Life Vinaya Master Hongjing come forth!" A white ox lowed aloud as it passed by. "Come forth, Past Life Kitchener Guangzhao!" A black ox also passed by lowing. "Labor Steward Jingben, come forth!" A lowing bullock came out. "Past Life Director of Affairs Fazhong come forth!" Another lowing bullock came out. Shide then led them off himself, saying to them as he did so, "You did not observe the Precepts in your past lives. You had human faces but the hearts of beasts, and so you have brought this misfortune on yourselves. Who else could you blame? Though the power of the Buddha is great, you have proved yourself unworthy of his grace."

1 Shide is probably criticizing the monks for continuing to manifest themselves as beings subject to karma, and hence to rebirth.

大眾驚訝忙然。因玆又報州縣。使令入州。不赴召命。盡代人仰。因此顯現。寺眾彷徨。咸歎菩薩來於人世。聊纂實錄。貴不墜爾。兼於土地堂壁上書語數聯。貴示後人。乃集語曰。

東洋海水清，
水清復見底，
靈源涌法泉，
斫水無刀痕。

我見頑嚚士，
燈心柱須彌。
寸樵煑大海，
甲扶大地石。

烝砂豈成飯，
磨甎將作鏡。
說食終不飽，
直須著力行。

The monks were confused by this, and once more they reported the matter to the district authorities. The authorities sent an order that Shide should come to the prefectural capital, but he did not obey this command. He had manifested in response to the reverence of others, but the temple monks had hesitated in recognizing him. Since all now marveled that a bodhisattva had come into the human world, the monks planned to compose a true record of what had happened so that they would no longer be remiss. They combined this record with various couplets Shide had written on the walls of local shrines, wishing to make it known to later generations. Here are the collected sayings:[1]

The water of the Great Ocean is clear;
And since it's clear, one can see to the bottom.
A dharma spring wells up from a sacred source;
Chop at the water—it leaves no marks.

I see a crude, self-satisfied man:
He's like a lampwick supporting Mount Sumeru,[2]
Or a splinter of firewood boiling the sea
Or a fish-scale supporting a mighty boulder.

Steaming sand will never produce food;
You're polishing a tile to make a mirror.
Just talking about food won't make you full;
You just have to apply some effort![3]

---

1 Most of these verses, like the ones attributed to Fenggan, fall into four-line units. Many of them repeat or adapt lines from both the Shide and Hanshan collections in an arbitrary way (as the editor mentions in a note appended to the beginning of SD 40). It may be possible that this "Record of Shide" originally circulated independent of the poetry collection and was inserted here later. It is also notable that, unlike the Fenggan note, it does not have Lüqiu Yin as its purported author.

2 This image is also found in SD 39.

3 This verse, which incorporates separate images from HS 97 and HS 213, seems self-contradictory.

恢恢大丈夫，
堂堂六尺士。
枉死埋冢間，
可惜孤標物。

不見日光明，
照耀於天下。
太清廓落洞，
明月可然貴。

余本住無方，
盤泊無為里。
時陟涅槃山，
徐步香林裏。

左手握驪珠，
右手執摩尼。
莫邪未足刃，
智劍斬六賊。

般若酒清泠，
飲啄澄神思。
余閑來天台，
尋人人不至。

Imposing, a great stalwart;
Impressive, a six-foot man.
Yet they die for naught and are buried in mounds;
How sad, their solitary markers!

Haven't you seen how the light of the sun
Illumines all the world below it?[1]
The great void of sky is broad and empty,
And the bright moon is worthy of reverence.

Where I dwell is Nowhere Place;
I linger in the village of Karmic Freedom.[2]
At times I climb Nirvana Hill,
Or stroll idly in Xianglin.[3]

Left hand grasps the dragon pearl,
Right hand holds the *maṇi* gem.
A blade beyond Moye's talents,
The sword of wisdom beheads the Six Bandits.[4]

How cold is the wine of wisdom!
Those who drink will clarify their divine thoughts.[5]
I came idly to Tiantai
Seeking for someone who did not come.

1 A variant of the opening of SD 41.
2 I read the variant 里 ("village") for the text's 理 ("principle") here and in SD 42.
3 With a minor change in the fourth line, these are the first four lines of SD 42.
4 Moye was a legendary swordsmith. These images are also found in SD 43.
5 Compare with SD 44.

寒山同為侶，
松風水月間，
何事最幽邃，
唯有遯居人。

悠悠三界主，
古佛路棲棲，
無人行至此。
今跡誰不躡，
旋機滯凡累。

可畏生死輪，
輪之未曾息。
嗟彼六趣中，
茫茫諸迷子。

人懷天真佛，
大寶心珠祕。
迷盲沈沈流，
汩沒何時出。

拾得自閭丘太守拜後。同寒山子把手走出寺。跡隱。後因國清僧登南峯采薪。遇一僧似梵儀。持錫入巖。挑鎖子骨而去。乃謂僧曰。取拾得舍利。僧遂白寺眾。眾方委拾得在此巖入滅。乃號為拾得巖。在寺東南隅。登山二里餘地。聊錄如前。貴示後人矣。

Hanshan became my companion,
Mid the pine breeze and the water-moon.
What matter is most hidden and remote?
Only becoming a recluse.

You multitudinous lords of the Three Realms!
The path of past Buddhas is drear and chill,[1]
And no one can walk it and reach them.
Who would not tread in their steps?
But all return to their devices, hobbled by mundane bonds.

How frightful the wheel of life and death!
One can never rest on it.
Alas, all those on the Six Courses,
The vast hordes of those who are lost.

People have within them the true Buddha,
A great treasure, a mind-jewel hidden away.
But they are lost and blind, sunk in the current,
Rolling about, and will never emerge.

After Governor Lüqiu took office, Shide fled the temple with Master Hanshan and disappeared. Later, some monks from Guoqing climbed a peak to the south to gather firewood, and they encountered a monk with an Indian demeanor, holding a ringed staff and entering a cliff. There he picked out some bones that were linked together with a chain.[2] As he left, he said to the monks, "I am taking the relics of Shide." The monks then reported this to the assembly. The assembly concluded that Shide had entered nirvana at this cliff, and they named it "Shide Cliff." It is located at a nook southeast of the temple, on some fallow land about two *li* up the mountain. They recorded this as they had with earlier events, wishing to make it known to later generations.

1 Compare with SD 32.

2 Relics consisting of linked bones occur in some Tang hagiographies and tales as marks of a bodhisattva.

SD 1

諸佛留藏經，
只為人難化。
不唯賢與愚，
4 箇箇心搆架。
造業大如山，
豈解懷憂怕。
那肯細尋思，
8 日夜懷姧詐。

SD 2

嗟見世間人，
箇箇愛喫肉。
椀楪不曾乾，
4 長時道不足。
昨日設箇齋，
今朝宰六畜。
都緣業使牽，
8 非干情所欲。
一度造天堂，
百度造地獄。
閻羅使來追，
12 合家盡啼哭。

DOI 10.1515/9781501501913-009,

SD 1

All the Buddhas have left us their scriptures
Only because humans are so hard to change.
Not only the worthy and the foolish—
Each one of us has a deceptive heart.
The karma we make is as huge as the hills,
Yet we hardly know that we should worry.
Never willing to look at things carefully,
Day and night we embrace sin and falsehood.

SD 2

I sigh to see men in the world,
Each one in love with eating flesh.
Their plates and bowls are never dry,
Yet always they complain of dearth.
Yesterday they held a feast for monks,[1]
This morning they slaughter beasts for food.
All because karma drives them there—
It's not what their nature desires!
For every deed worthy of Heaven
A hundred are worthy of Hell.
Then Yama's guards will drag them off,[2]
While their families sob in mourning.

1 A vegetarian feast give for monks was a standard way for lay believers to acquire merit.

2 Yama is the king of the Hell realms.

鑪子邊向火，
鑊子裏澡浴。
更得出頭時，
16 換却汝衣服。

SD 3

出家要清閑，
清閑即為貴。
如何塵外人，
4 却入塵埃裏。
一向迷本心，
終朝役名利。
名利得到身，
8 形容已顦顇。
況復不遂者，
虛用平生志。
可憐無事人，
12 未能笑得尔。

They'll face the fire of furnace Hells,
And they'll bathe in their boiling pots.
And just when they escape from them,
16 They're given a new suit to wear.[1]

SD 3

In "leaving the home" you must be pure and calm:
Purity and calm must be valued.
What's the point for a man "beyond the dust"
4 To enter again into dust and filth?
Once his essential mind loses its way,
All day he toils for fame and profit.
And when fame and profit come to him
8 His body will be worn out.
Even more true for those who don't follow the Path,
Vainly employing their whole lives' will.
How sad—the one who has no affairs[2]
12 Can't bring himself to laugh at you.

1 That is, reincarnated.
2 The truly enlightened practitioner.

SD 4

養兒與娶妻，
養女求媒娉。
重重皆是業，
4 更殺眾生命。
聚集會親情，
總來看盤飣。
目下雖稱心，
8 罪簿先注定。

SD 5

得此分段身，
可笑好形質。
面貌似銀盤，
4 心中黑如漆。
烹猪又宰羊，
誇道甜如蜜。
死後受波吒，
8 更莫稱冤屈。

SD 4

Raise a son: you find him a good wife;
Raise a daughter: you seek a good match.
Heap upon heap of karmic burdens:
And still you take the lives of living beings.[1]
You bring your relatives together,
And all of them come to look at the feast.
Though what they see will please their hearts,
A record is made of their sinful deeds.

SD 5

This body obtained—with its share of karma:
Delightful, what a fine physical form!
With face as lovely as a silver plate,
But black as lacquer in the heart.
Boil a pig, slaughter a sheep:
Boast that they taste as sweet as honey.
But after death, you receive your torture:
Don't complain then that you've been wronged!

1 Looking after a child involves enough planning and stress to produce bad karma; but if you slaughter animals at the wedding feast, you make it worse.

SD 6

佛哀三界子，
總是親男女。
恐沈黑暗阬，
示儀垂化度。
盡登無上道，
俱證菩提路。
教汝癡眾生，
慧心勤覺悟。

SD 7

佛捨尊榮樂，
為愍諸癡子。
早願悟無生，
辦集無上事。
後來出家者，
多緣無業次。
不能得衣食，
頭鑽入於寺。

SD 6

Lord Buddha laments those of the Three Realms—
For all of them are his own sons and daughters.
He fears that they're sunk in a pit of darkness,
So shows various forms to convert and to save.
Then all shall climb the unsurpassable Way,
All realize the road of Enlightenment.
I instruct you, you foolish living beings:
With a wise heart you should toil to awaken.

SD 7

The Buddha cast aside honor, glory and pleasure,
For he pitied all ignorant beings.
Early he vowed to realize Non-Birth,
So to manage the greatest matter of all.
But later all those who "leave their homes,"
Mostly because they have no trade
And cannot obtain clothing or food,
Hide their heads inside a temple.[1]

1 Present-day monks become so only to support themselves and not to engage in compassionate practice.

SD 8

嗟見世間人，
永劫在迷津。
不省這箇意，
修行徒苦辛。

SD 9

我詩也是詩，
有人喚作偈。
詩偈總一般，
讀時須子細。
緩緩細披尋，
不得生容易。
依此學修行，
大有可笑事。

SD 10

有偈有千萬，
卒急述應難。
若要相知者，
但入天台山。

SD 8

Alas, I see the people of the world:
For endless kalpas, losing their path.
They don't examine this Meaning;[1]
Their practice is only bitter toil.

SD 9

Yes, my poems are poems—
Though some might call them *gāthas*.
Poem or *gātha*—it's all the same;
4 When you read verse you must be careful.
Slowly pore over them as you read,
And don't let yourself get lazy.
Rely on this to study cultivation,
8 And you'll find it quite delightful!

SD 10

There are millions of *gāthas*:
It should be hard to explain them too quickly.
So if you want someone who understands you,
4 Just enter the Tiantai Mountains.

1 The true significance of the Dharma. Compare HS 105 and HS 172.

巖中深處坐，
說理及談玄。
共我不相見，
對面似千山。

SD 11

世間億萬人，
面孔不相似。
借問何因緣，
致令遣如此。
各執一般見，
互說非兼是。
但自修己身，
不要言他己。

SD 12

男女為婚嫁，
俗務是常儀。
自量其事力，
何用廣張施。
取債誇人我，
論情入骨癡。

On a cliff sit in an isolated place,
Discuss principle and debate mysteries.
But if we don't share our vision,
Though face to face, it's though a thousand hills part us.

SD 11

All the billions of people in the world:
None of their faces are the same.
I ask what are the causes and conditions
That have brought them to be so?
Each one holds to his own views;
They argue with each other on what is wrong and right.
Instead, just cultivate your own self;
You mustn't speak of "him" or "me."

SD 12

Men and women go off and get married,
Their social duties a constant habit.
But you should measure your own capacities;
Useless to advertise yourselves.
Collecting debts, boasting of your contests,
In affairs, you're stupid right to the bone.

殺他雞犬命，
身死墮阿鼻。

SD 13

世上一種人，
出性常多事。
終日傍街衢，
不離諸酒肆。
為他作保見，
替他說道理。
一朝有乖張，
過咎全歸你。

SD 14

我勸出家輩，
須知教法深。
專心求出離，
輒莫染貪淫。
大有俗中士，
知非不愛金。
故知君子志，
任運聽浮沈。

You'll take the lives of chickens and dogs,
And when you die, fall into Avīci Hell.

SD 13

One kind of man in the world:
He's always meddling to an extreme.
All day hanging around on the street,
Never leaving the wine shops.
If you act as his guarantor
And talk to him about the rules,
When one day he commits a crime,
Blame for his actions will fall on you.

SD 14

I urge those who leave the household:
You must profoundly know the Teachings.
Concentrate wholly on liberation,
Never stain yourselves with greed or lust.
There are always some laymen
Who know wrong and do not cherish gold.
So you should know the will of a good man:
Follow fate, rise and fall with the flood.

SD 15

寒山住寒山，
拾得自拾得。
凡愚豈見知，
豐干却相識。
見時不可見，
覓時何處覓。
借問有何緣，
向道無為力。

SD 16

從來是拾得，
不是偶然稱。
別無親眷屬，
寒山是我兄。
兩人心相似，
誰能徇俗情。
若問年多少，
黃河幾度清。

SD 15

Cold Mountain lives on Cold Mountain;
Shide's always Shide.
How could the common fools know us by sight?
But Fenggan knows us well.
When they look for us they can't see us;
When they peer at us we can't be found.
If you ask us what karmic bonds we share:
On *our* path we generate no karma.

SD 16

Once upon a time I was a foundling,[1]
So my name isn't coincidental.
And I have no other kith and kin;
Cold Mountain is my brother.
The two of us are alike in mind:
Neither can follow a vulgar nature.
And if you ask how old we are:
How many times has the Yellow River been clear?

1 "Picked up," a reference to Shide's name.

SD 17

若解捉老鼠，
不在五白猫。
若能悟理性，
那由錦繡包。
真珠入席袋，
佛性止蓬茅。
一群取相漢，
用意總無交。

SD 18

運心常寬廣，
此則名為布。
輟己惠於人，
方可名為施。
後來人不知，
焉能會此意。
未設一庸僧，
早擬望富貴。

SD 17

As for knowing how to catch a rat—
You won't get that from a calico cat.
As for waking to Reality—
You can't pull that out of a fine silk purse.
The true pearl is inside a straw bag,
The Buddha Nature stops in a rustic hut.
All of you fellows who judge by appearance:
Your efforts are utterly pointless.

SD 18

The impulse for giving should always be generous;
This might be called "charity";
Being selfless, but kindly to others;
This could be termed "giving."[1]
Lately, people don't know this;
How could they understand this idea?
Even before they've brought in some common monk,
They already hope for wealth and status.[2]

1 Compare the structure here to HS 79.

2 Well-off families patronized monks in the hope to obtain merit that would bring positive material benefit; this is not the proper motive that should underlie *dāna* or *bushi*, one of the Six Perfections (the two characters *bu* and *shi* are translated as "charity" and "giving" here).

SD 19

獼猴尚教得，
人何不憤發。
前車即落阬，
4 後車須改轍。
若也不知此，
恐君惡合殺。
比來是夜叉，
8 變即成菩薩。

SD 20

君不見
三界之中紛擾擾，
只為無明不了絕。
一念不生心澄然，
無去無來不生滅。

SD 21

故林又斬新，
剡源谿上人。
天姥峽關嶺，
4 通同次海津。

SD 19

Even a monkey can be taught,
So why should men not rouse themselves?
If the cart in front falls into a pit,
The cart behind should change its path.
If you can't understand this,
Then I'm afraid your wickedness will bring your demise.[1]
Those who were demons previously,
Can change and become bodhisattvas!

SD 20

Haven't you seen—
The Three Realms thrown into turmoil,
All because the ignorant don't know how to stop.
If a single thought does not arise, the mind is clarified:
No going and no coming, no arising and no destruction.

SD 21

The home forest is refreshed again
For the man standing by Shan Creek's source.
Tianmu Mountain: its passes, gorges, peaks
Press hard upon the ocean side.[2]

---

1 Compare HS 144, ll. 15–18.

2 Tianmu Mountain and neighboring Shan Creek are part of the Tiantai range. They are particularly famous in literature through the poetry of Xie Lingyun and Li Bai.

灣深曲島間，
淼淼水雲雲。
借問嵩禪客，
8 日輪何處暾。

SD 22

自笑老夫筋力敗，
偏戀松巖愛獨遊。
可歎往年至今日，
任運還同不繫舟。

SD 23

一入雙溪不計春，
鍊暴黃精幾許斤。
鑪竈石鍋頻煑沸，
4 土甑久烝氣味珍。
誰來幽谷餐仙食，
獨向雲泉更勿人。
延齡壽盡招手石，
8 此棲終不出山門。

In the depths of the bay, the far off isles,
The vast waters lost in mist.
I ask Meditation Master Song:
Where is the sun that shines so dim?[1]

SD 22

A laugh at myself, an old man with sinews powerless;
But with fond affection for piney cliffs and a love of lonely rambling.
What's amazing: from former years up until today,
Turning myself over to fate just like an unmoored boat.[2]

SD 23

Once I entered Double Springs, countless years went by;[3]
There I refined and dried many a pound of Solomon's Seal.[4]
In stove and furnace, in stoneware cauldron I boiled it several times;
In earthen crocks I steamed it long until vapor and taste were refined.
Who comes now to my remote valley to taste this immortal food?
I'm alone amid the clouds and the streams, there's no one here at all.
My long life will come to an end here by the Beckoning Stone;[5]
Roosting here, I'll never depart the temple's mountain gate.

1 This poem is somewhat garbled. Xiang Chu cites an apocryphal Chan story about a recluse named Song Toutuo 嵩頭陀, who awakened Shanhui 善慧 to his true nature while he was fishing.

2 The two lines of the last couplet are taken from HS 123 and HS 182.

3 This refers to two streams in the Tiantai area: Youxi 猶溪 and Xiandaxi 縣大溪.

4 Literally, "Yellow Essence": a combination of polygonatum species used as a cure in traditional Chinese medicine.

5 Zhiyi 智顗 (the founder of Tiantai Buddhism) dreamed that he saw a magical monk beckoning him by a boulder at Tiantai. He took this as a sign that he should move there.

SD 24

躑躅一群羊，
沿山又入谷。
看人貪竹塞，
4 且遣豺狼牧。
元不出孳生，
便將充口腹。
從頭喫至尾，
8 ⿰飠內⿰飠內無餘肉。

SD 25

銀星釘稱衡，
綠絲作稱紐。
買人推向前，
4 賣人推向後。
不顧他心怨，
唯言我好手。
死去見閻王，
8 背後插掃箒。

SD 24

A flock of sheep is wandering about,
Is following the hills and entering valleys.
Their shepherd is set on his gambling games[1]
When he encounters jackals and wolves in pursuit.[2]
They weren't raised by the wolves at all,
But now they fill wolves' mouths and bellies!
Devoured from their heads down to their tails,
With not a leftover in sight.

SD 25

Silver weights fastened from the steelyard,
Green threads serve as the steelyard cord.[3]
Buyers push themselves in front,
Sellers thrust themselves behind.
No heed have they for the wrongs of others,
Only say, "I'm pretty good at this."
After they die, they'll see King Yama;
He'll stick them with a broom-tail.[4]

1 Accepting the variant 博簺 for 竹塞.
2 Accepting the variant 逐 for 牧.
3 This is a description of the measuring scales used in the marketplace.
4 Cause them to reincarnate as animals.

SD 26

閉門私造罪，
準擬免災殃。
被他惡部童，
4 抄得報閻王。
縱不入鑊湯，
亦須臥鐵牀。
不許雇人替，
8 自作自身當。

SD 27

悠悠塵裏人，
常道塵中樂。
我見塵中人，
4 心多生愍顧。
何哉愍此流，
念彼塵中苦。

SD 26

You shut the door, commit your sins in private,
Intending that way to avoid calamity.
But the boy who copies your evil deeds
Writes it all down, reports it to Yama.[1]
Even if you don't enter the boiling cauldron,
You'll be laid out on the iron bed.
You can't hire someone to take your place—
Your deeds will be on your own head.

SD 27

How many the people in the dust,
Always talking about their dusty delights!
I see these people in the dust,
And so often I feel sorry for them.
How can I feel sorry for people like that?
I remember that there's pain in that dust as well.

1 A Buddhist folk belief holds that there are two scribes whose job it is to write down both the good and evil deeds of each person and to report them to Yama, king and judge of the underworld.

SD 28

無去無來本湛然，
不居內外及中間。
一顆水精絕瑕翳，
光明透滿出人天。

SD 29

少年學書劍，
叱馭到荊州。
聞伐匈奴盡，
婆娑無處遊。
歸來翠巖下，
席草翫清流。
壯士志未騁，
獼猴騎土牛。

SD 30

三界如轉輪，
浮生若流水。
蠢蠢諸品類，
貪生不覺死。

SD 28

No goings, no comings, originally tranquil;
No dwelling within or without, or at the point between.
A single crystal of purity without flaw or crack;
Its light penetrates and fills up the worlds of men and gods.

SD 29

In my youth I studied books and swordsmanship;
Bent on saving the state, I drove toward Jingzhou.[1]
There I heard the campaigns against the Xiongnu were done,
So I lingered, aimless, no place to go.
I went home again to the foot of azure cliffs,
Made grass my mat, delighted in the clear streams.
Before a man in his prime can pursue his will,
He's reduced to a monkey riding a clay ox.

SD 30

The Three Realms are like a turning wheel;
This floating life like flowing water.
All living beings are squirming together,
Greedy for life and ignorant of death.

---

1 Jingzhou was the district in the central Yangtze valley that often served as a strategic linchpin for military campaigns. This resonates oddly with the next line, with its mention of the Xiongnu; but the poet is likely gesturing toward places where military activity is common. "Bent on saving the state I drove" is literally "I shouted at the carriage driver." The allusion here refers to Wang Zun of the Han dynasty, who commanded his driver to take him over a dangerous mountain road while he served as Regional Inspector of Yizhou. His predecessor, Wang Yang, had refused to take the same road, because he felt he should preserve his own life for the sake of his ancestors. The term came to be used to describe those who placed loyalty to the state above their own lives and private concerns.

汝看朝垂露，
能得幾時子。

SD 31

閑入天台洞，
訪人人不知。
寒山為伴侶，
松下噉靈芝。
每談今古事，
嗟見世愚癡。
箇箇入地獄，
早晚出頭時。

SD 32

古佛路淒淒，
愚人到却迷。
只緣前業重，
所以不能知。
欲識無為理，
心中不掛絲。
生生勤苦學，
必定覩天師。

Just look at the morning dew—
How long can it last?

SD 31

I idly enter Tiantai grottoes
To visit someone, though no one knows.
Hanshan is my companion;
Under the pines we dine on magic fungi.
Always we chat about matters new and ancient,
Sighing that the world is so foolish.
One by one they enter into hell,
And when will they ever get out of it?

SD 32

The path of past Buddhas is drear and chill,
Fools who come to it are lost.
All because their karmic burden is heavy,
They are unable to learn of it.
If you want to know how to be free of karmic action,
No garments may hang about your heart.
From life to life study with all your might,
Then you'll certainly see the Celestial Teacher.

SD 33

各有天真佛，
號之為寶王。
珠光日夜照，
玄妙卒難量。
盲人常兀兀，
那肯怕災殃。
唯貪淫泆業，
此輩實堪傷。

SD 34

出家求出離，
哀念苦眾生。
助佛為揚化，
令教選路行。
何曾解救苦，
恣意亂縱橫。
一時同受溺，
俱落大深阬。

SD 33

Each has a naturally authentic Buddha;
We name it the Prince of Jewels.
The light of this pearl shines day and night;
Its dark mysteries impossible to measure.
But the blind are always muddled,
Unwilling to fear disaster and calamity.
Only greedy for a karma of excess,
This gang is really pitiable.

SD 34

Those who have left their home seek escape,
And think with pity of the suffering of living things.
They help the Buddhas to spread the message of salvation,
Causing all to choose the right path to take.
But when have they ever understood how to relieve suffering?
Doing as they please, wildly going in all directions.
All at once they will drown together,
All falling in the great deep Pit.

SD 35

常飲三毒酒，
昏昏都不知。
將錢作夢事，
4 夢事成鐵圍。
以苦欲捨苦，
捨苦無出期。
應須早覺悟，
8 覺悟自歸依。

SD 36

雲山疊疊幾千重，
幽谷路深絕人蹤。
碧澗清流多勝境，
時來鳥語合人心。

SD 37

後來出家子，
論情入骨癡。
本來求解脫，
4 却見受驅馳。

SD 35

Always they drink the wine of Three Poisons,
Benighted, all of them unaware.
Using money to pay for their dreams,
Dreams that turn into an Iron Cage.[1]
With suffering they try to relieve suffering,
Yet this relief will never take place.
From the start they ought to struggle to wake up—
Awakening that comes from Taking Refuge.[2]

SD 36

Cloudy mountains, rank upon rank, how many thousand layers!
Secluded valley—the road deep, cut off from human traces.
The jade stream flows clearly through a realm of many marvels;
From time to time, the chattering of birds matches with my mood.

SD 37

Monks of this latter time:
To tell the truth, they're stupid to the bone.
Originally they sought Liberation,
But now they bustle about at the tasks they get.

---

1 A term for Hell.
2 For Taking Refuge, see HS 1 and note.

終朝遊俗舍，
禮念作威儀。
博錢沽酒喫，
8 翻成客作兒。

SD 38

若論常快活，
唯有隱居人。
林花長似錦，
4 四季色常新。
或向巖間坐，
旋瞻見桂輪。
雖然身暢逸，
8 却念世間人。

SD 39

我見出家人，
總愛喫酒肉。
比合上天堂，
4 却沉歸地獄。

All day traveling to laymen's homes,
Paying respects, chanting sutras, performing rituals.
They get their pay, then go drinking,
Acting just like hired laborers.

SD 38

If you discuss what'll make you always happy,
There's only the life of the recluse.
The trees in flower are always like brocade;
In all four seasons, their colors are ever renewed.
Sometimes I sit on the cliffs,
Gazing long at the cinnamon moon-wheel.[1]
Although the body's free and easy,
Yet I still think of people in the world.

SD 39

I see those who have become monks:
All of them love to drink wine and eat meat.
Originally they acted with Heaven-bound conduct,
But then sank into a path toward Hell.

1 A reference to the cinnamon tree that grows on the moon. Compare HS 68.

念得兩卷經,
欺他道鄽俗。
豈知鄽俗士,
8 大有根性熟。

下五首與前長偈語句同

SD 40

我見頑鈍人,
燈心柱須彌。
蟻子齧大樹,
4 焉知氣力微。
學咬兩莖菜,
言與祖師齊。
火急求懺悔,
8 從今輒莫迷。

SD 41

君見月光明,
照燭四天下。
圓暉掛太虛,
4 瑩淨能蕭灑。

Chanting their two chapters of sutras,
They cheat the people of the marketplace.
But how could they know that among those marketplace people
Are many who have roots of merit that have matured?

The following five poems have lines in common with the long gātha *quoted above.*[1]

SD 40

I see those foolish men,
A tiny wick supporting Mt. Sumeru.
Ants gnawing away at a mighty tree,
Unaware how weak their power is.
Training to eat their stalks of grass,
Saying they're the same as their masters.
You must seek to confess your sins right now!
Don't always be lost as you are now.

SD 41

Have you seen the brilliance of the moon?
A shining candle illuminating all the earth.
Its round radiance hangs in the Great Void,
Sleek and clean, as clear as this.

1 That is, the verse that comes at the end of the biographical note on Shide.

人道有虧盈，
我見無衰謝。
狀似摩尼珠，
光明無晝夜。

SD 42

余住無方所，
盤泊無為里。
時陟涅槃山，
或翫香林寺。
尋常只是閑，
言不干名利。
東海變桑田，
我心誰管你。

SD 43a

左手握驪珠，
右手執慧劍。
先破無明賊，
神珠自吐燄。

People say it waxes and wanes,
But I see that it has no fading or withering.
Its form is like the *maṇi* pearl;
Bright light no matter day or night.

SD 42

Where I dwell is Nowhere Place;
I linger in the village of Karmic Freedom.
At times I climb Nirvana Hill,
Or enjoy myself in temples of fragrant trees.[1]
Typically I find nothing but leisure,
My speech indifferent to fame and profit.
As the eastern sea turns to mulberry fields,[2]
My mind, who will bother with you then?

SD 43a[3]

Left hand grasps the dragon pearl,
Right hand holds the sword of wisdom.
First I smash the robbers of ignorance—
Then the divine pearl emits a blaze of its own.

1 Possibly alluding to the comparison of the scent of fragrant trees to the teaching of the Dharma that is occasionally found in Buddhist texts.

2 A common expression referring to the inevitable change of the world over time.

3 SD 43 is without a doubt two separate poems. The first four lines are rather close rhetorically to the quatrain HS 299. The second four lines (which have nothing in common with the first four) begin with a lament for human folly—the most common recurring opening in the corpus.

SD 43b

傷嗟愚癡人，
貪愛那生猒。
一墮三途間，
始覺前程險。

SD 44

般若酒泠泠，
飲多人易醒。
余住天台山，
凡愚那見形。
常遊深谷洞，
終不逐時情。
無思亦無慮，
無辱也無榮。

此下與寒山詩大同小異語意相涉

SD 45

自從到此天台寺，
經今早已幾冬春。
山水不移人自老，
見却多少後生人。

SD 43b

Alas, how sad these fools!
They never grow tired of their covetousness.
Once they've fallen into the three evil paths,
They'll first know the dangers of their former course.

SD 44

How clear and cold is the wine of wisdom!
Those who drink deep will easily sober up.
I live at Tiantai Mountain—
4 How could I reveal myself to the foolish and common?
I often ramble in deep valleys and caves,
Never pursue the style of the time.
No worries and no concerns,
8 No shame and no glory either.

The poems below share their meanings with some of Hanshan's poems; they are largely the same, with small differences.

SD 45

From when I arrived at this Tiantai temple
Until now, I've already lived several winters and springs.
The landscape never changes, but people do grow old;
And now I see quite a few people younger than me.[1]

1 This is almost identical to HS 212. One wonders whether the only significant change ("realm" in HS, "temple" in SD) occurred because Shide was said to reside at Guoqing Temple.

SD 46

平生何所憂，
此世隨緣過。
日月如逝波，
光陰石中火。
任他天地移，
我暢巖中坐。

SD 47

嗟見多知漢，
終日枉用心。
岐路逞嘍囉，
欺謾一切人。
唯作地獄滓，
不修來世因。
忽爾無常到，
定知亂紛紛。

SD 46

What do I have to worry about in this existence?
I pass through this world following my karma.
Days and months pass like departing waves,
Time is just a flash from a flint stone.
Let Heaven and Earth change as it may,
But I'll delight in sitting here on my cliff.[1]

SD 47

I sigh to see those know-it-alls
Who vainly employ their mind all day,
Showing off their clever words at the crossroads,
Cheating everyone they meet.
They only become the dregs of Hell,
Don't cultivate the karma of the life to come.
When Impermanence comes upon them,
Certainly things will be thrown into chaos.[2]

1 Almost identical to ll. 3–8 of HS 171.
2 The same as HS 238 with minor variants.

SD 48

迢迢山徑峻，
萬仞險隘危。
石橋莓苔綠，
時見白雲飛。
瀑布懸如練，
月影落潭暉。
更登華頂上，
猶待孤鶴期。

SD 49

松月冷颼颼，
片片雲霞起。
匼匝幾重山，
縱目千萬里。
谿潭水澄澄，
徹底鏡相似。
可貴靈臺物，
七寶莫能比。

SD 48

Far far away, on mountain range steep,
And ten thousand fathoms high through a blocked precipice:
The moss grows green on Stony Bridge,
And sometimes I see white clouds drift by.
A waterfall hangs like a bolt of silk,
And moon's reflection sinks in the pool's light.
Again I climb Hua Peak—
Still waiting for a meeting with a lone crane.[1]

SD 49

The pine-tree moon is windblown and chill;
Shred by shred the roseate clouds rise.
The many layers of hills, clustered together,
Stretch to vision's limit for countless miles.
The valley pool water is clear
Like a mirror to its very depths.
The mind is a thing to be treasured—
How could a Seven-Jeweled Pagoda compare?[2]

1 That is, recognized by the Transcendents as one of their own.
2 A version of HS 264, with the first couplet moved to end and with variants.

SD 50

世有多解人，
愚癡學閑文。
不憂當來果，
4 唯知造惡因。
見佛不解禮，
覩僧倍生瞋。
五逆十惡輩，
8 三毒以為鄰。
死去入地獄，
未有出頭辰。

SD 51

人生浮世中，
箇箇願富貴。
高堂車馬多，
4 一呼百諾至。
吞併他田宅，
準擬承後嗣。
未逾七十秋，
8 冰消瓦解去。

SD 50

There are men with "great understanding"
Who foolishly study idle texts.
They do not worry about future results,
Only know how to create evil causes.
When they see the Buddha they can't pay him homage;
When they view a monk they grow even more angry.
The Five Perversions, the Ten Evil Acts,
The Three Poisons they take as neighbors.
And once they die, they enter Hell,
And they'll never emerge again.[1]

SD 51

Human life in this floating world:
Everyone wants to be rich:
With lofty hall, many horses and carriages,
A hundred assents to every summons.
Swallowing up others' fields and homes,
Planning to pass it on to descendants.
But before seventy autumns have passed,
The ice melts and the tiles shatter.[2]

1 A version of HS 91. The third couplet is close to the third couplet of HS 137.
2 Lines 4, 7, and 8 appear with slight changes in HS 85.

SD 52

水浸泥彈丸，
思量無道理。
浮漚夢幻身，
4 百年能幾幾。
不解細思惟，
將言長不死。
誅剝壘千金，
8 留將與妻子。

SD 53

雲林最幽棲，
傍澗枕月谿。
松拂盤陀石，
4 甘泉涌凄凄。
靜坐偏佳麗，
虛巖曚霧迷。
怡然居憩地，
8 日

以下缺

SD 52

It's like water soaking mud clods:
When you think about it, it makes no sense.
Like floating froth this illusory dream body;
Out of a hundred years how long can it last?
You don't know how to think deeply about it—
Just say that you'll live forever.
You scrape together your pile of gold
Merely to leave it to your wife and kids.

SD 53

Cloudy forest—the most secluded place to rest;
I keep to the stream, rest on the moonlit creek.
Pine trees brush the level stone,
Sweet springs well up in clarity.
I calmly take pleasure, only favoring beauty here,
Lost in the shrouding mists on this empty cliff.
I joyfully take my rest in this place,
The sun . . .[1]

The rest of the text is missing.

1 Nearly identical to ll. 3–6 of HS 267.

SD 54

可笑是林泉，
數里少人煙。
雲從巖嶂起，
瀑布水潺潺。
猿啼暢道曲，
虎嘯出人間。
松風清颯颯，
鳥語聲關關。
獨步繞石澗，
孤陟上峰巒。
時坐盤陀石，
偃仰攀蘿沿。
遙望城隍處，
惟聞鬧喧喧。

此首係別本增入

SD 54

How delightful this forest stream—
For several miles no smoke from human fires.
Clouds arise from cliffs and steeps,
While water murmurs in the torrent.
Gibbons chatter, singing a song of the Way;
Tigers roar as they come out among men.
The clear pine-wind whistles and roars,
And the speech of birds twitters around me.[1]
Alone, I tread round the stony creek,
Solitary, climb the peaks and hills.
At times I sit on the level stones;
Looking skyward I ascend, clambering up vines.
I gaze afar at the city walls
And only hear their clamor and din.

This poem has been added from another edition.

1 These four lines also appear in HS 165. See also the note to line 3 of that poem.

www.ingramcontent.com/pod-product-compliance
Lightning Source LLC
Chambersburg PA
CBHW060755310726
48980CB00002B/104

* 9 7 8 1 5 0 1 5 1 0 5 6 4 *